DRACOFORMES

serpents of stress relief

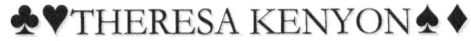

♣♥THERESA KENYON♠♦

This coloring book is dedicated to fire. And kitties.

CONTENTS

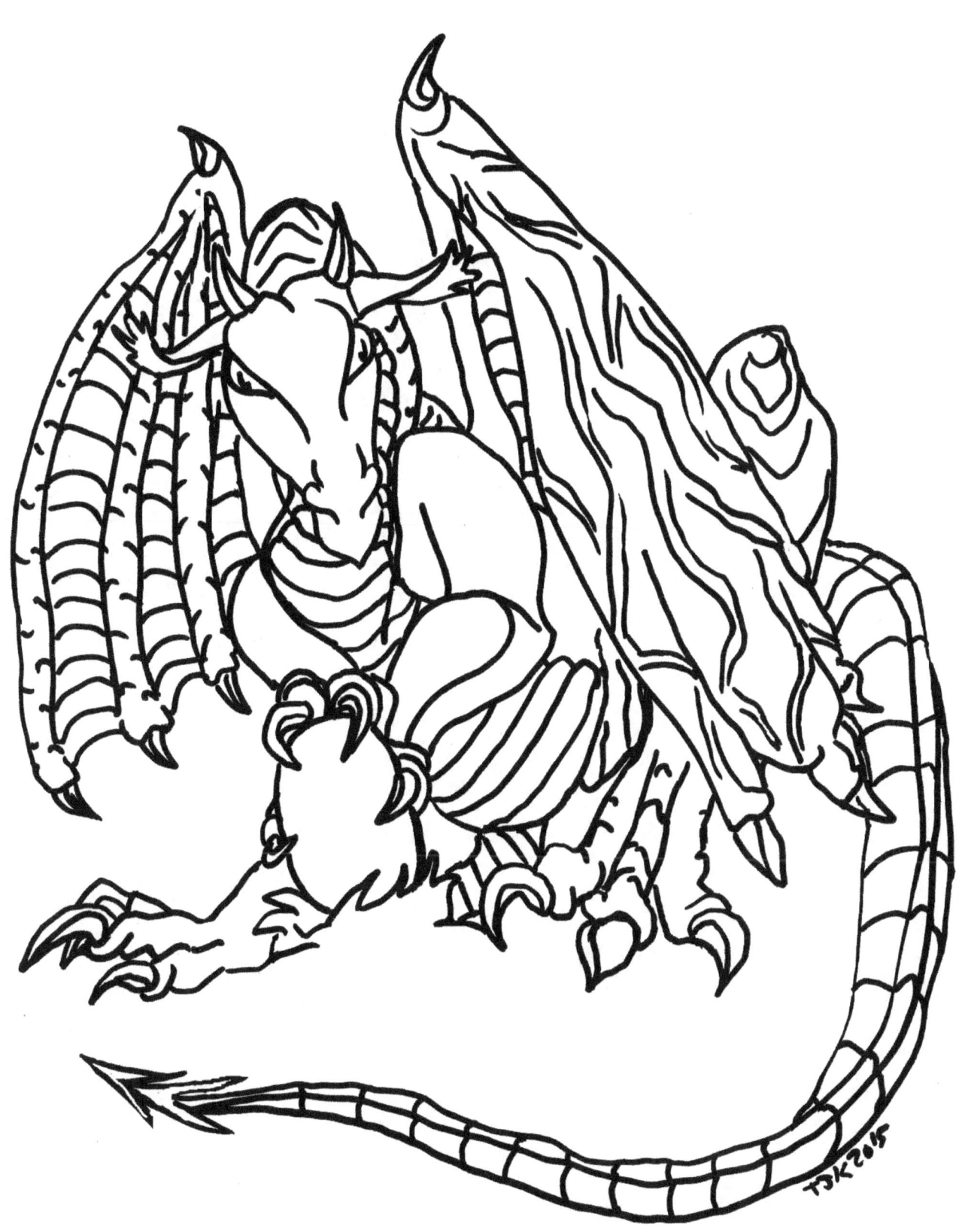

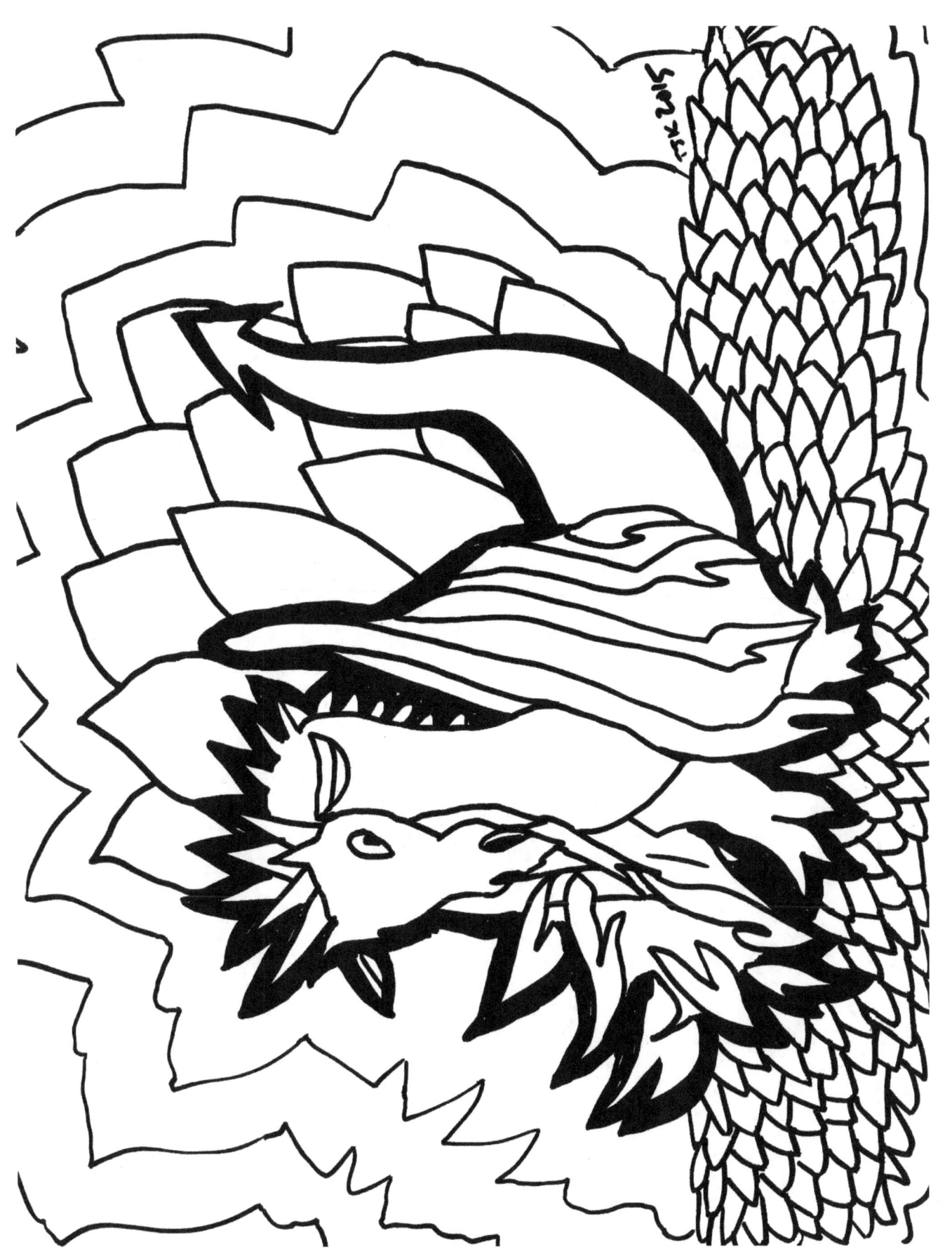

3

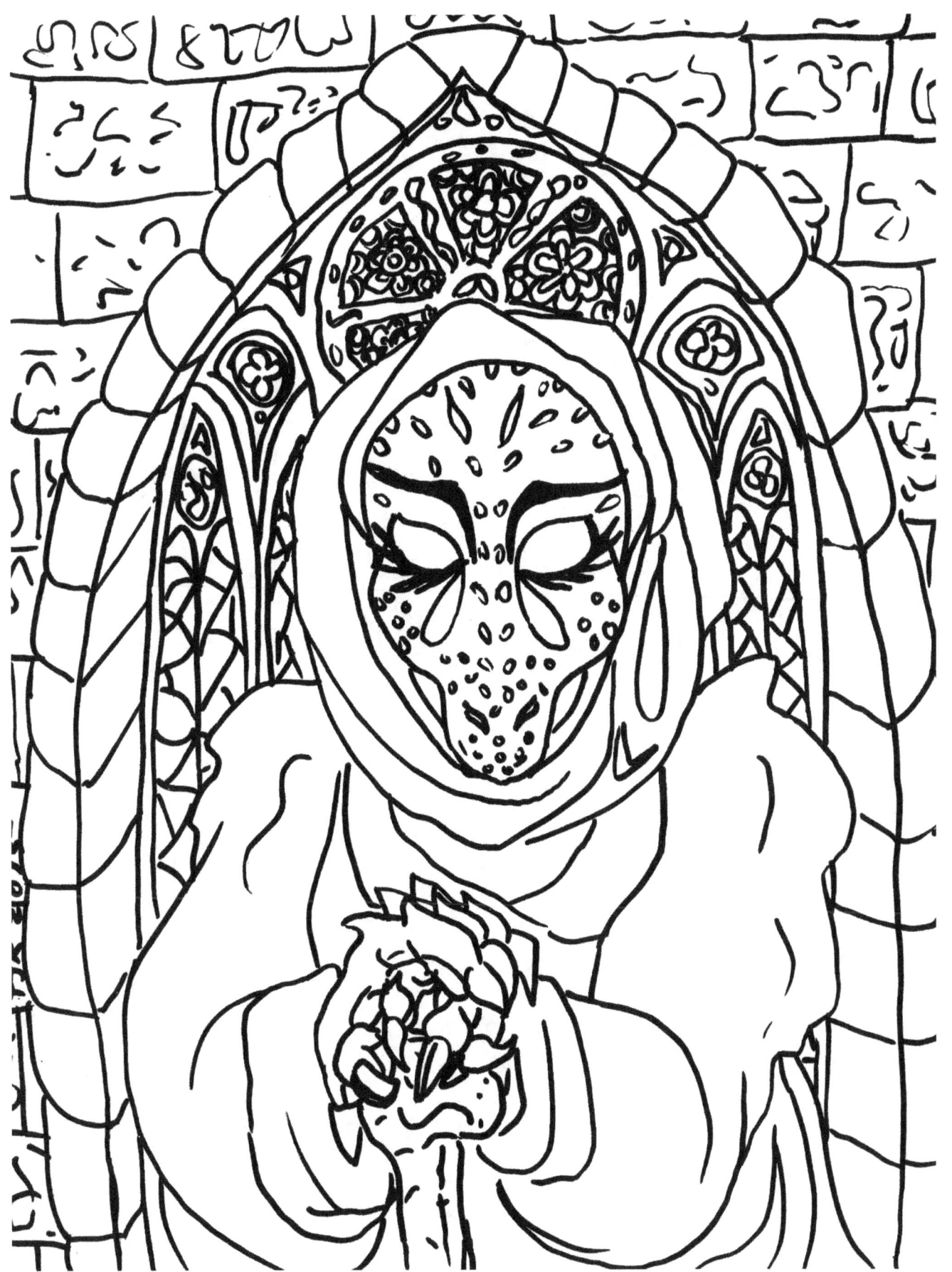

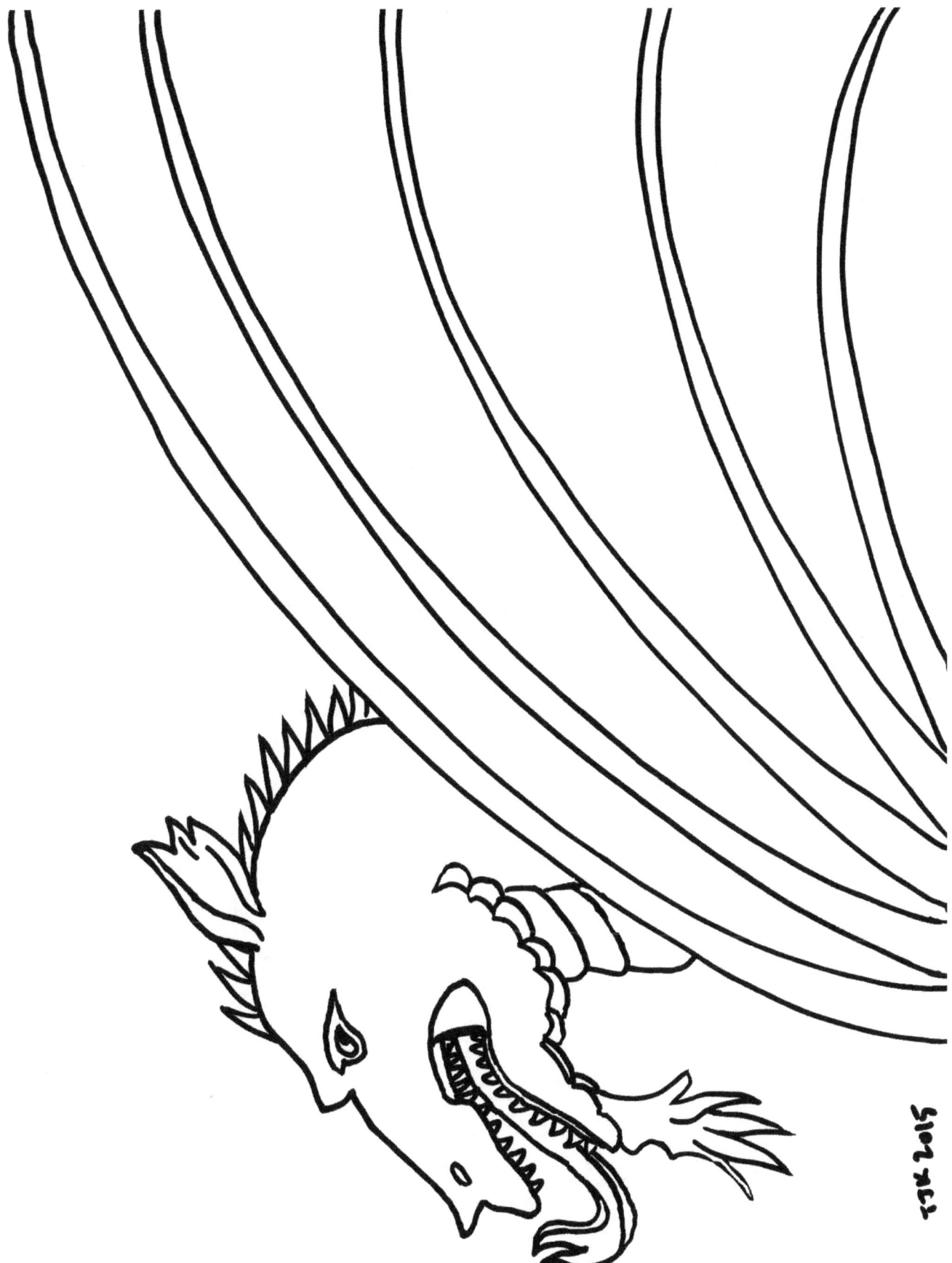

7

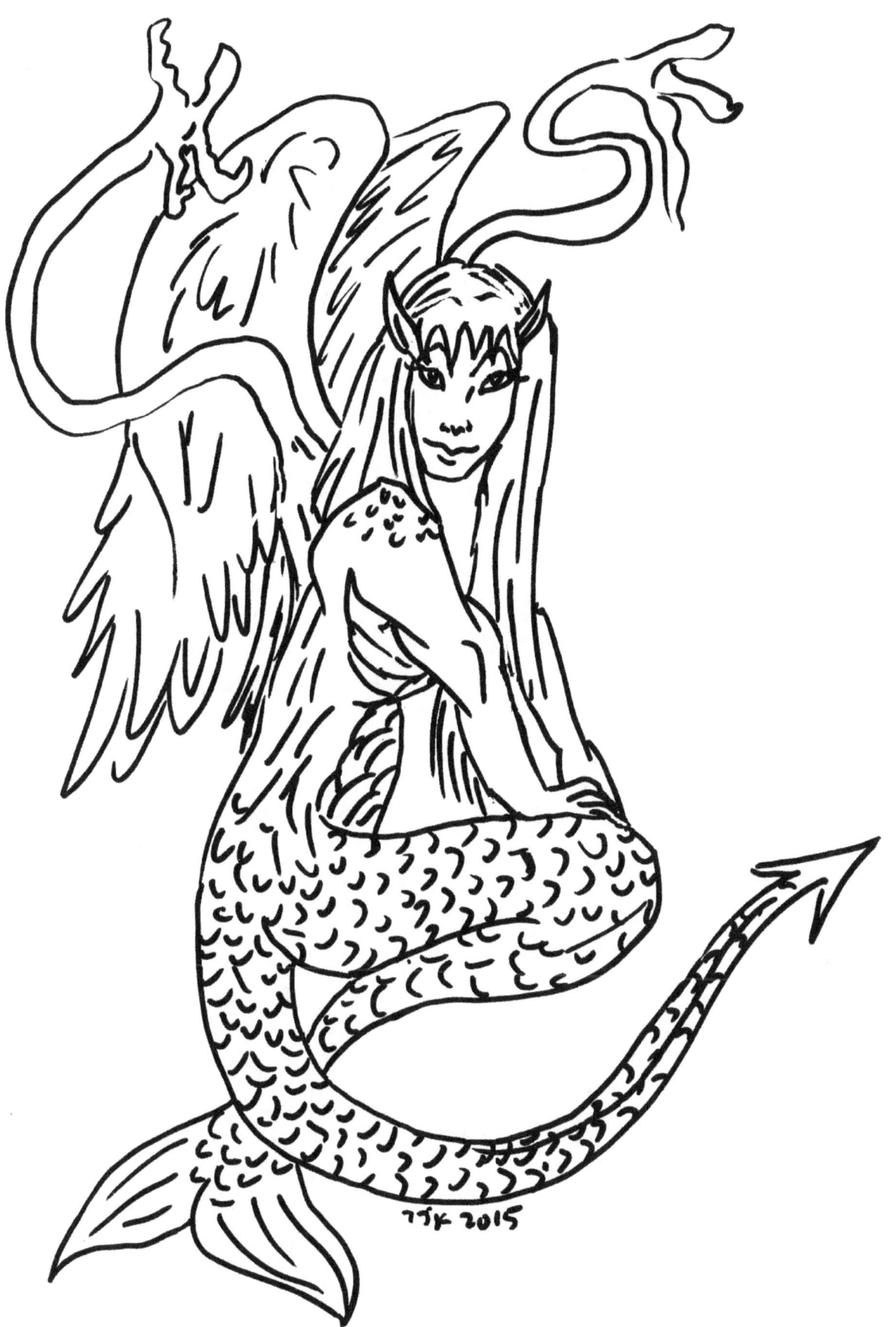

9

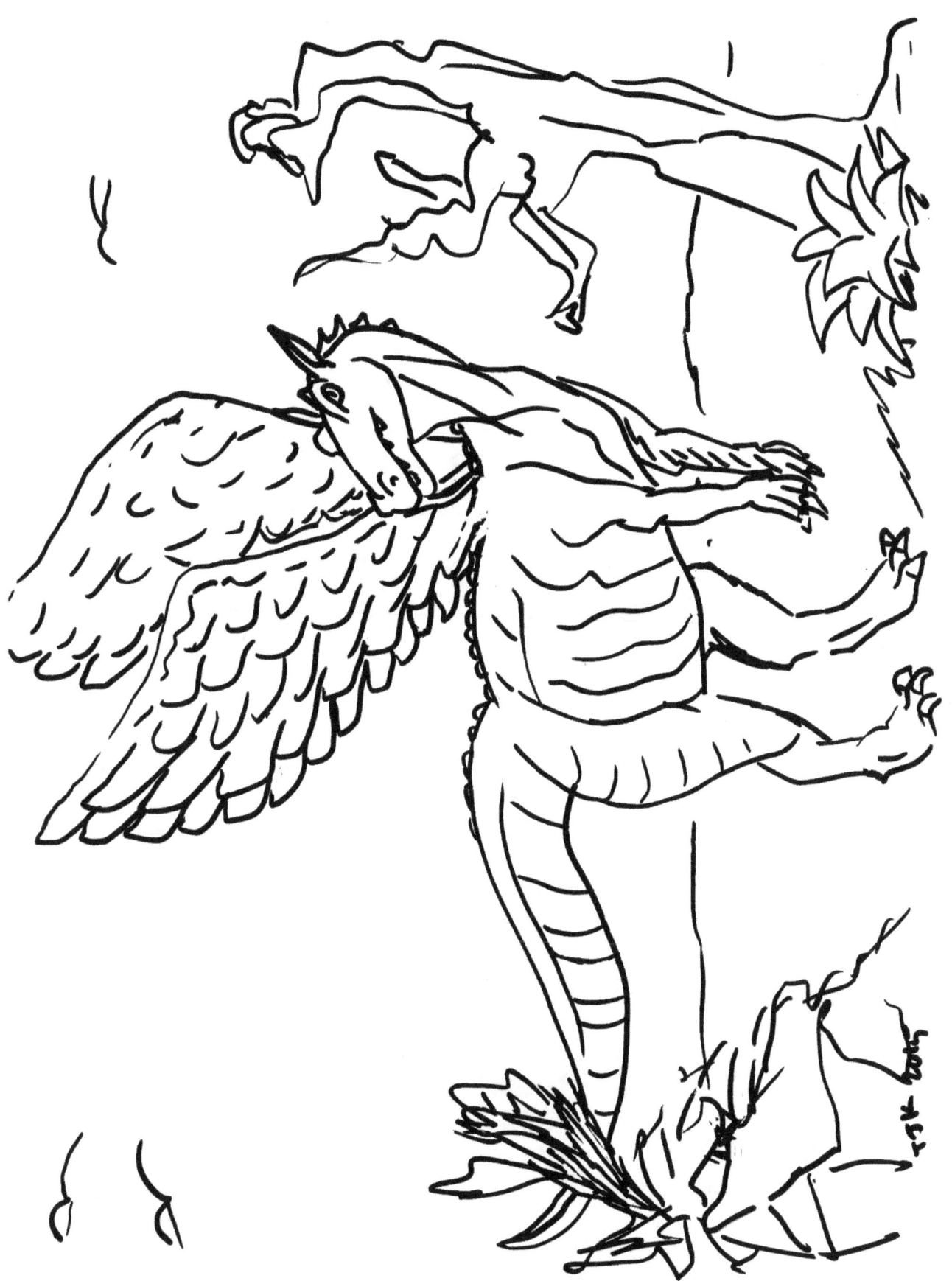

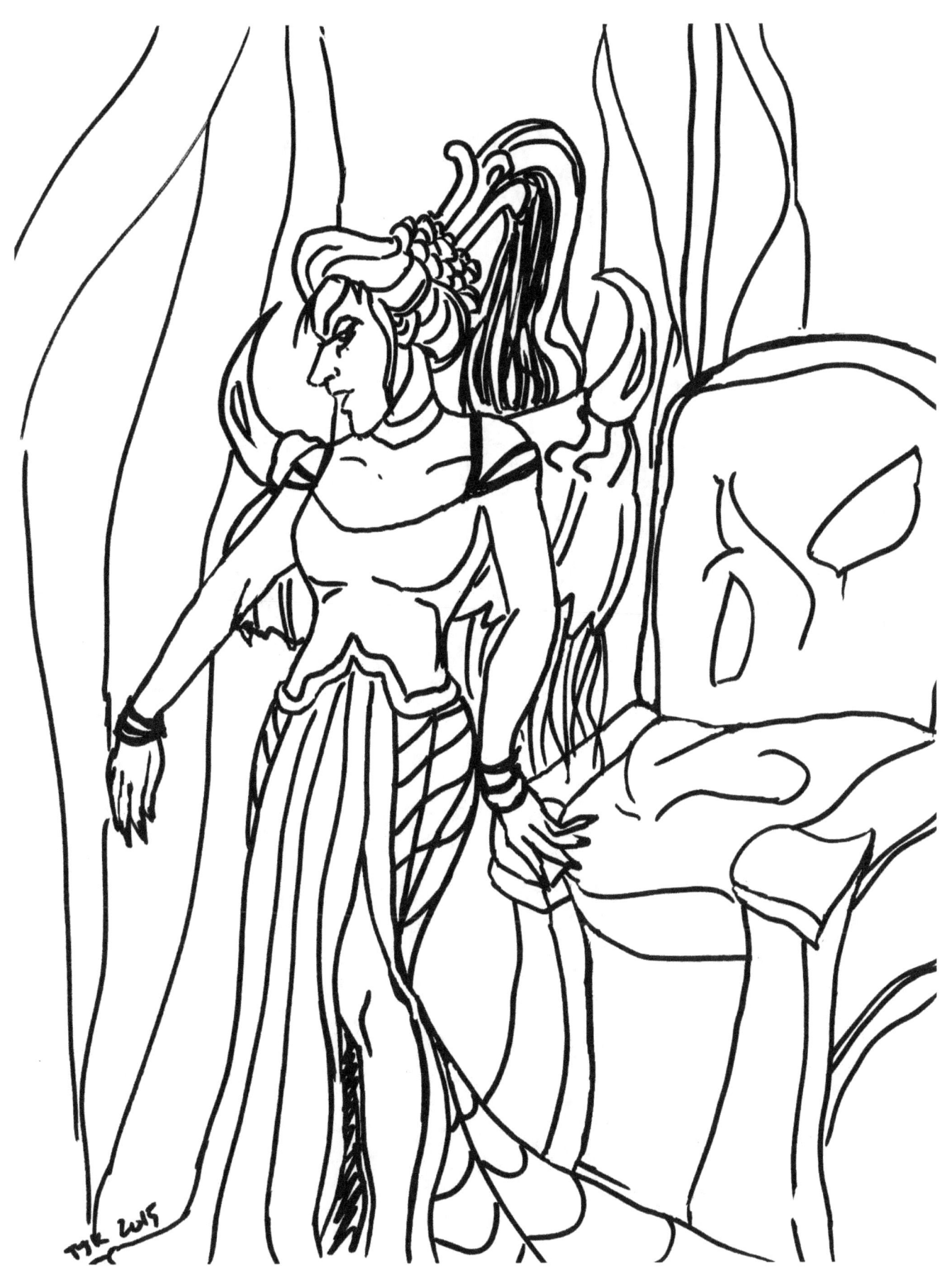

14

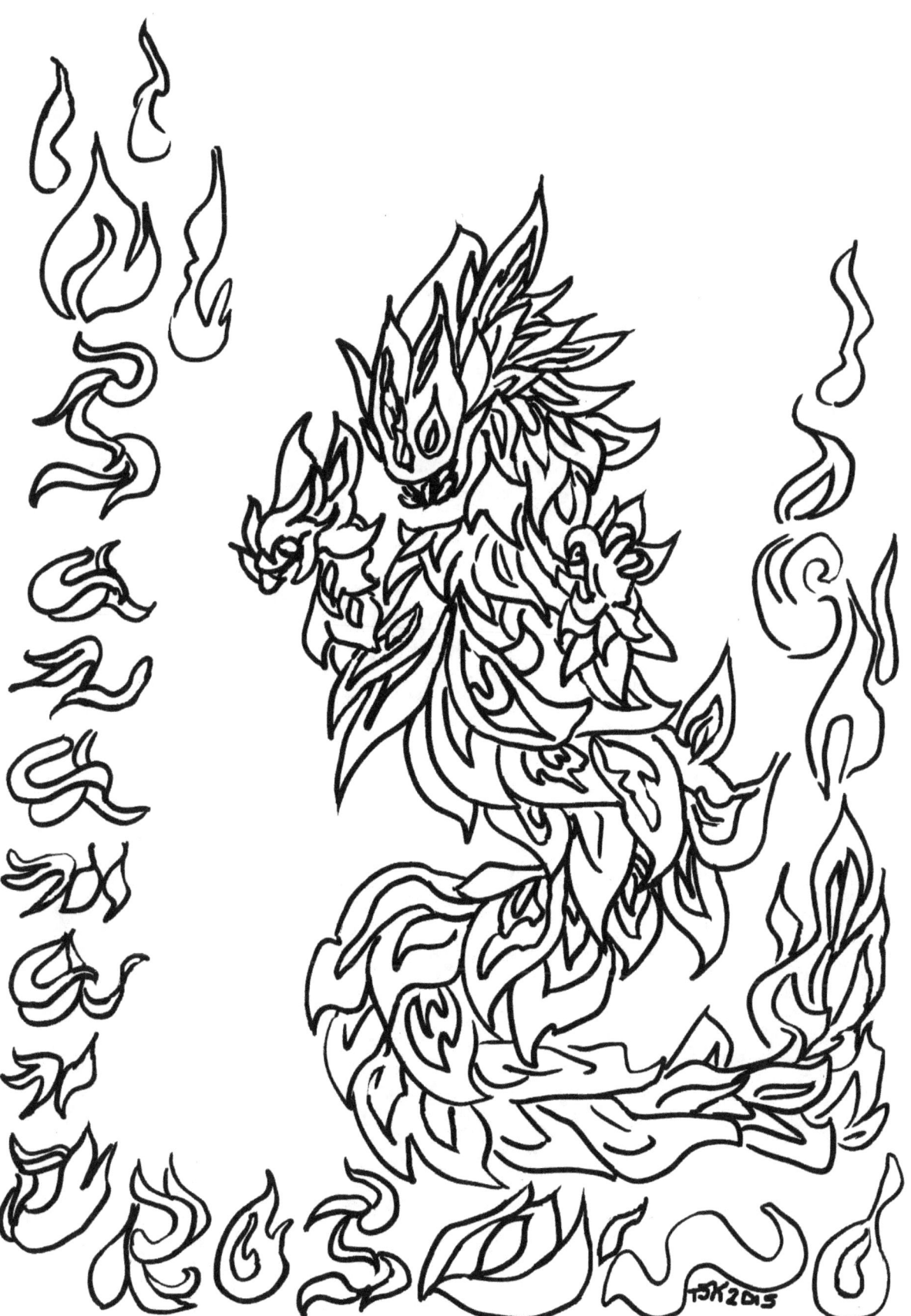

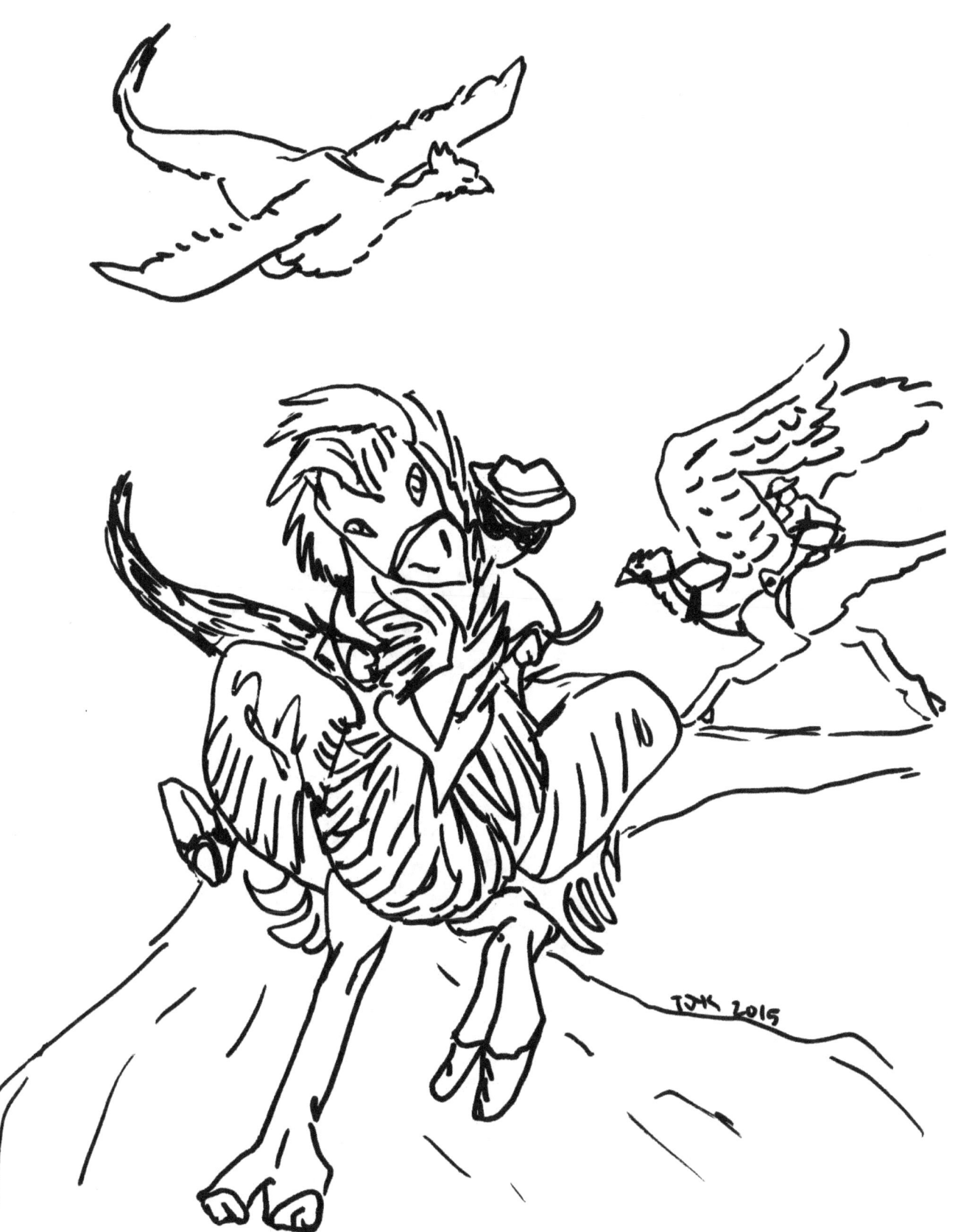

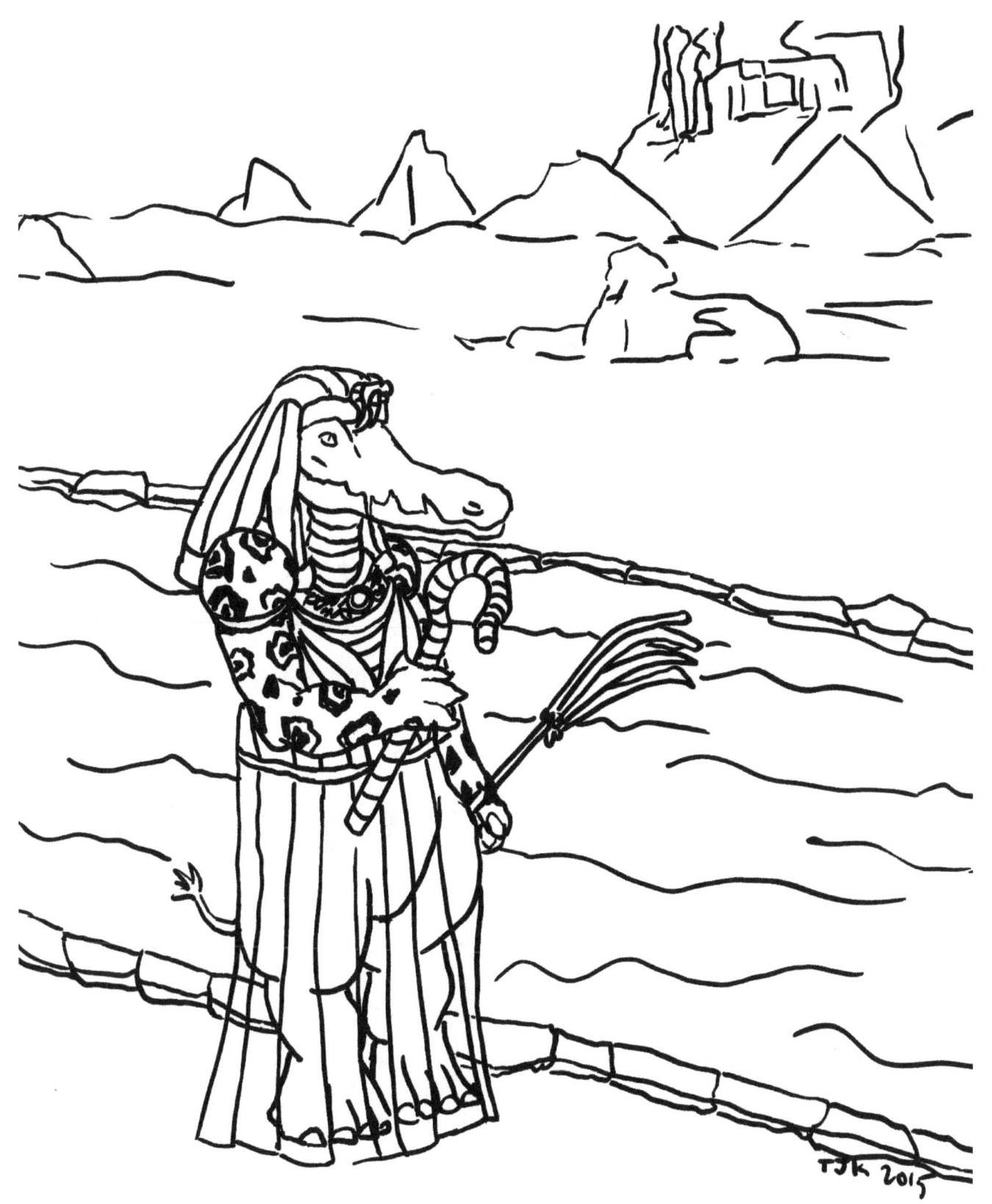

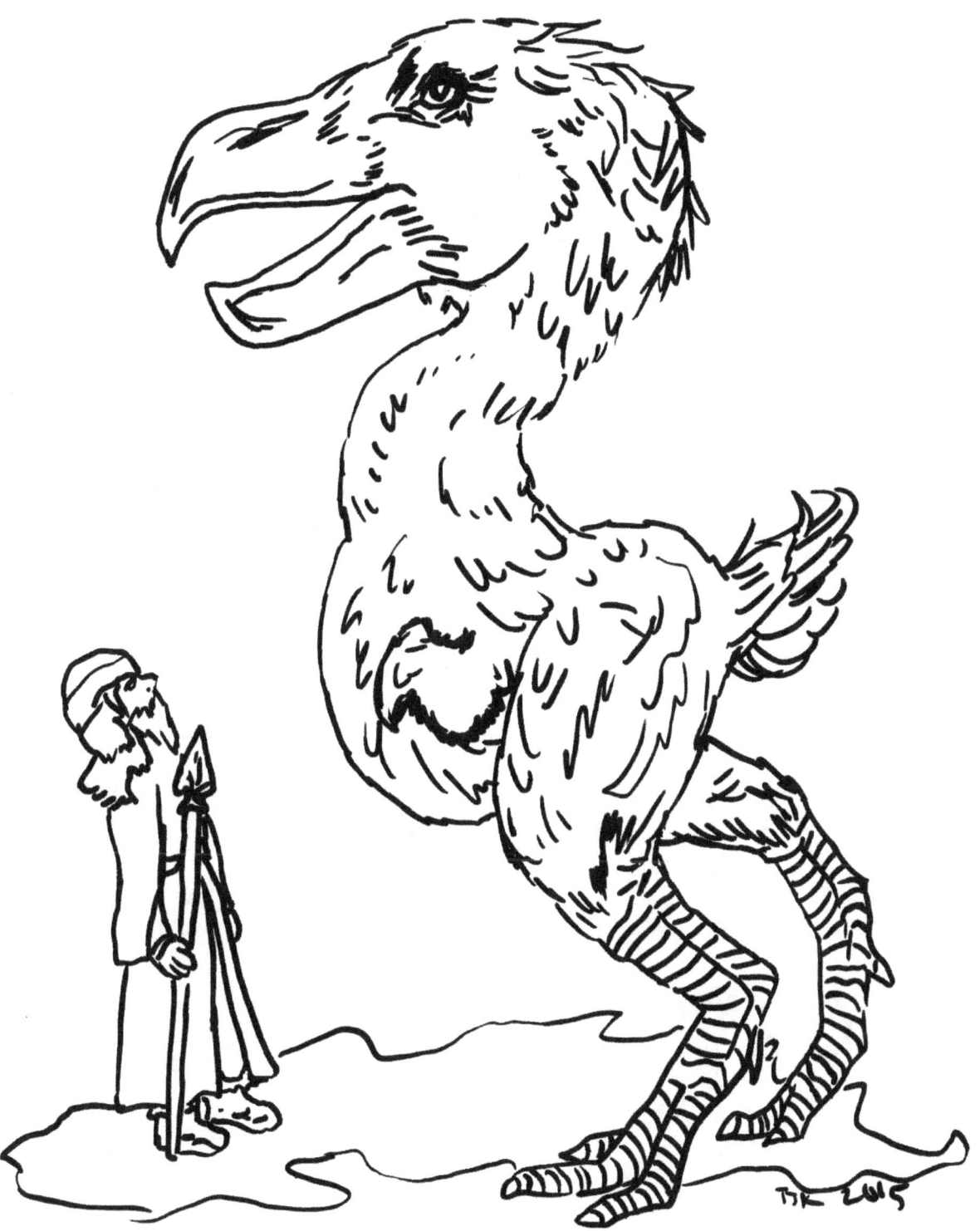

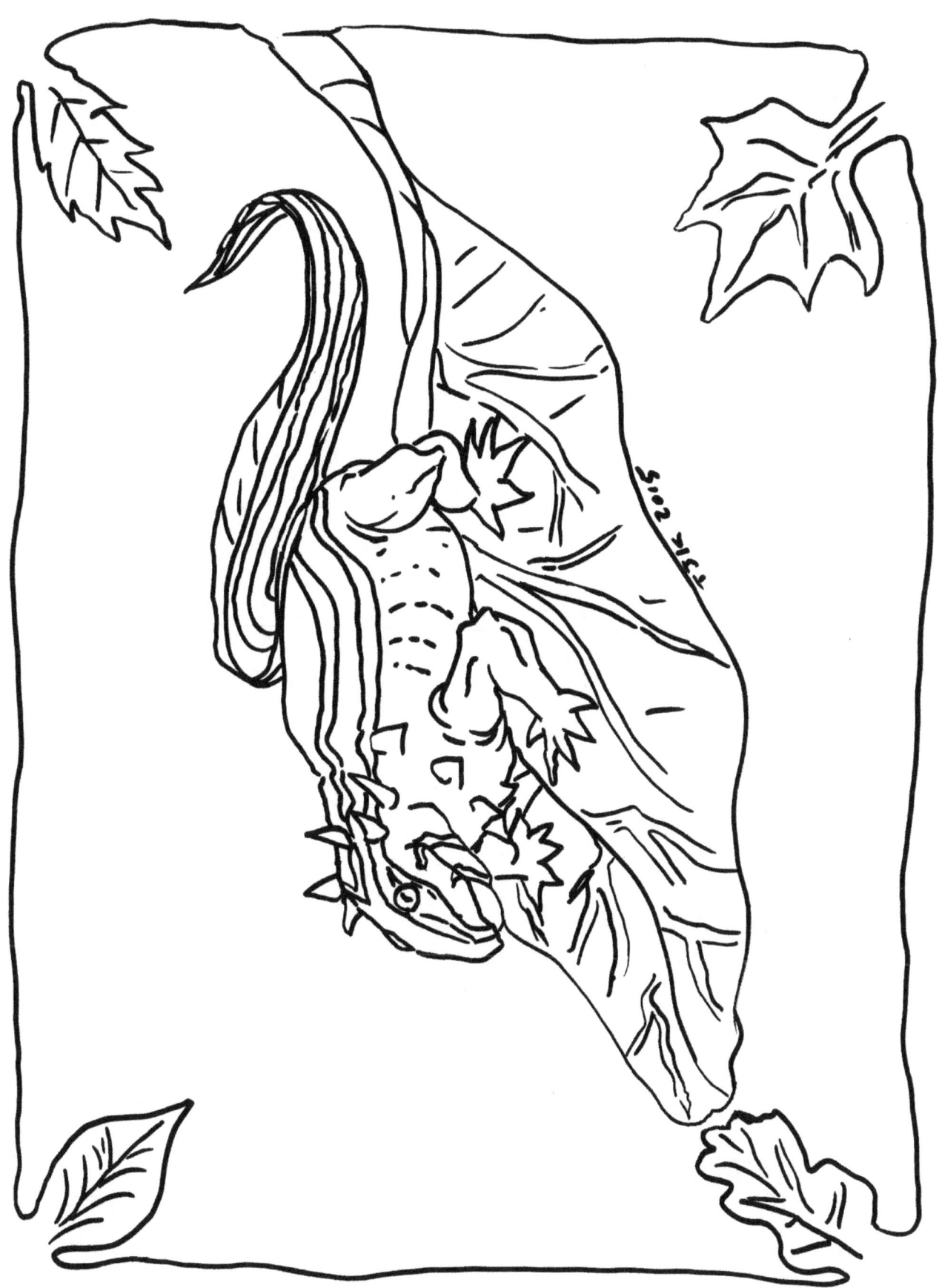

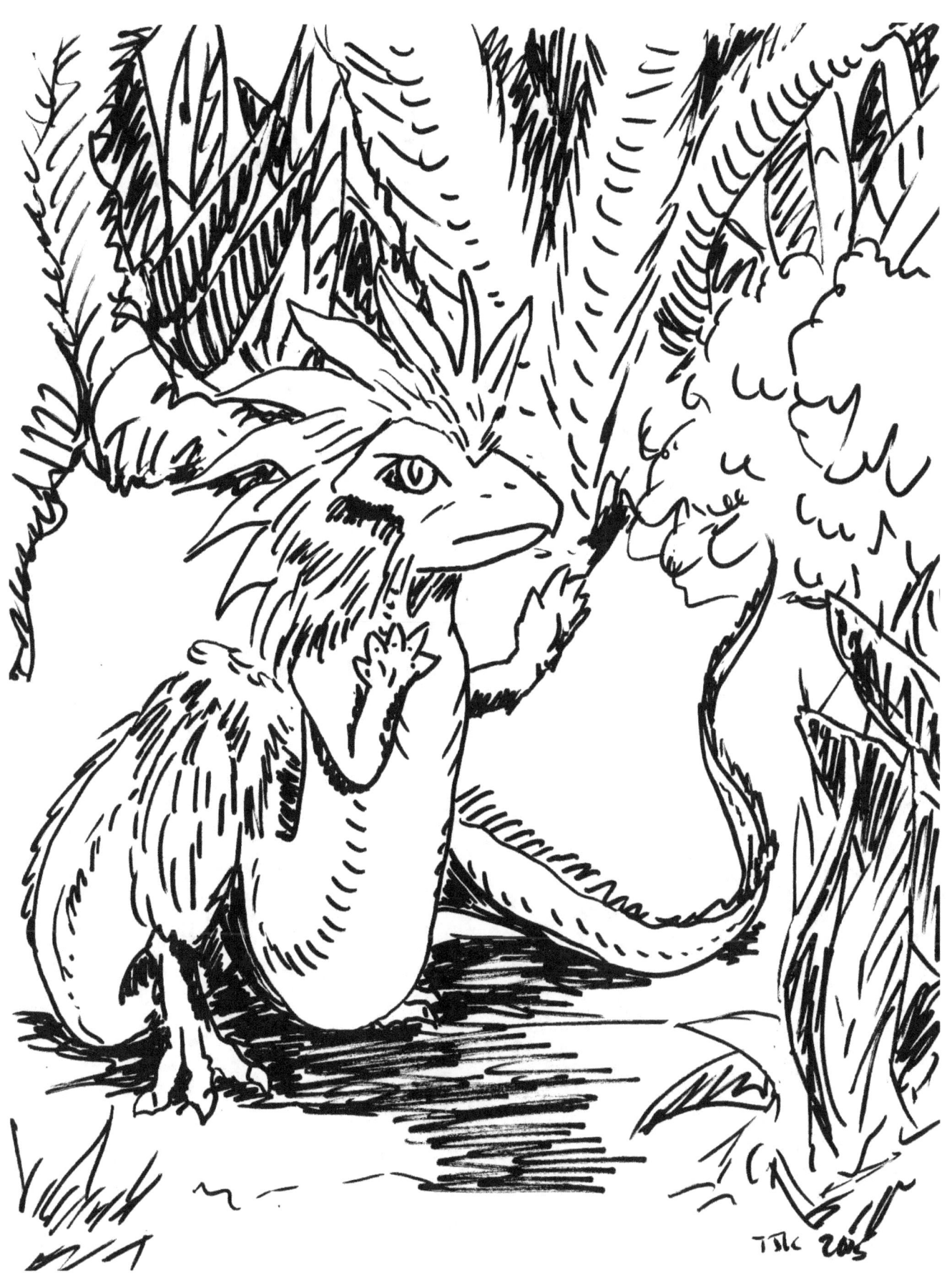

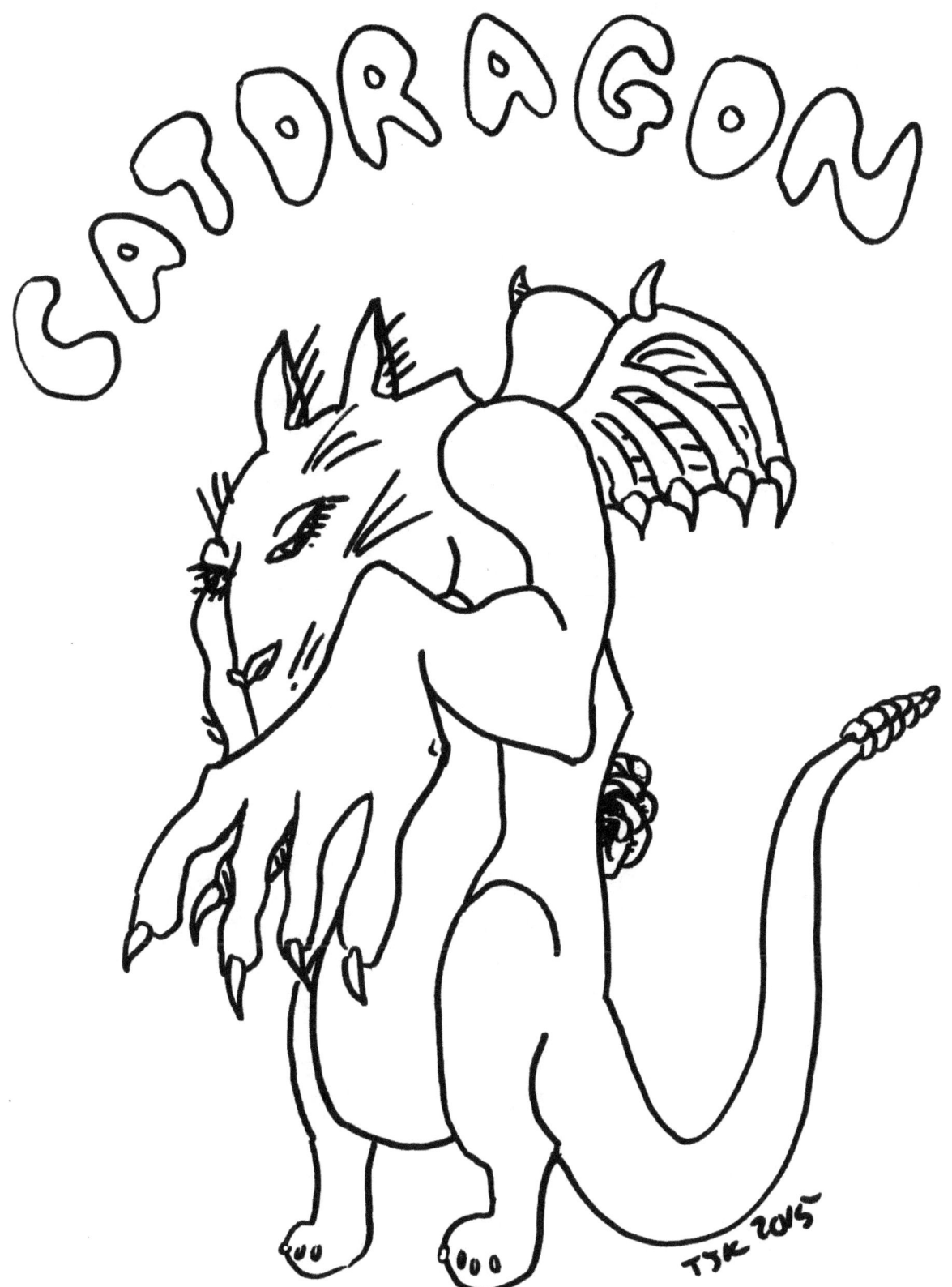

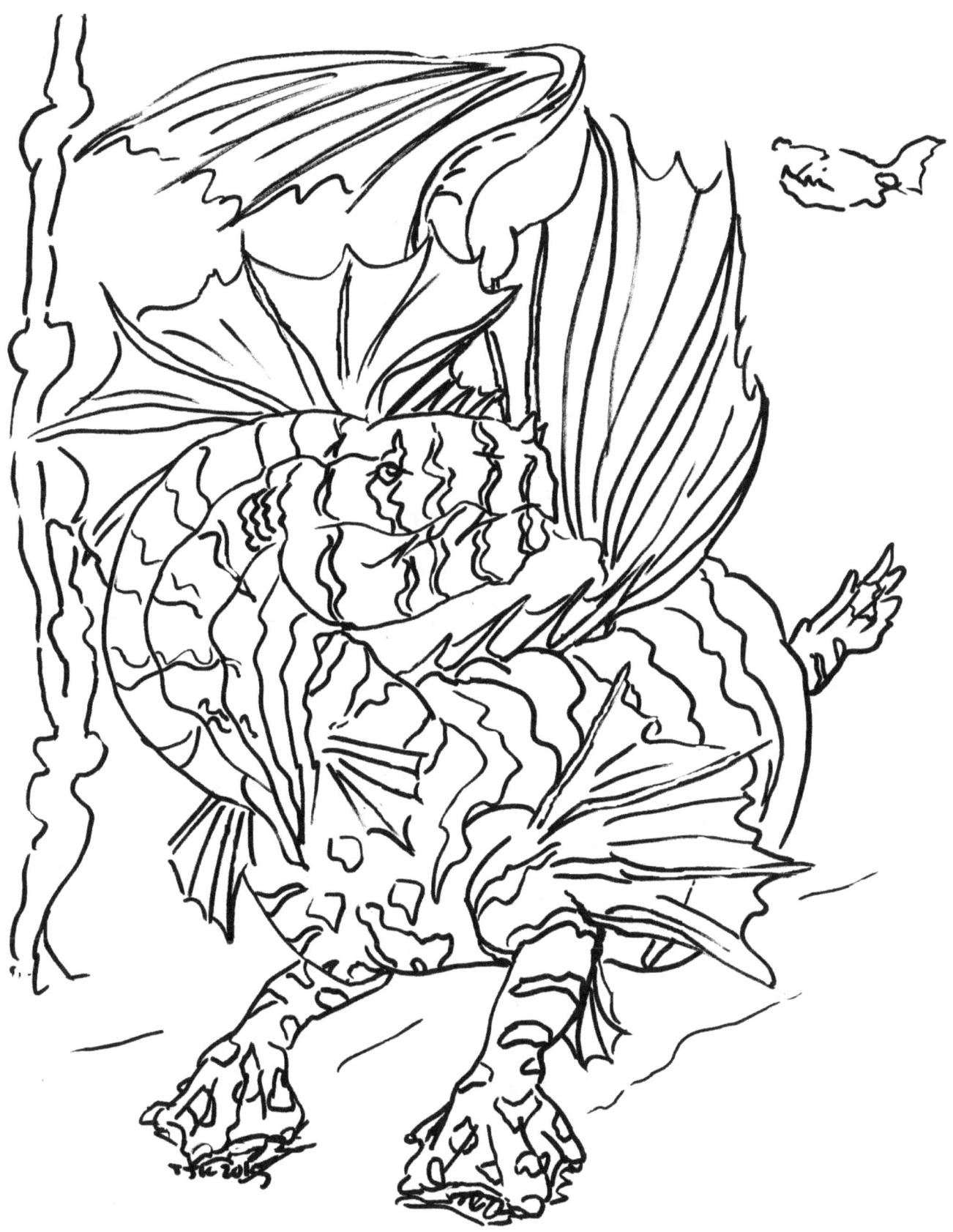

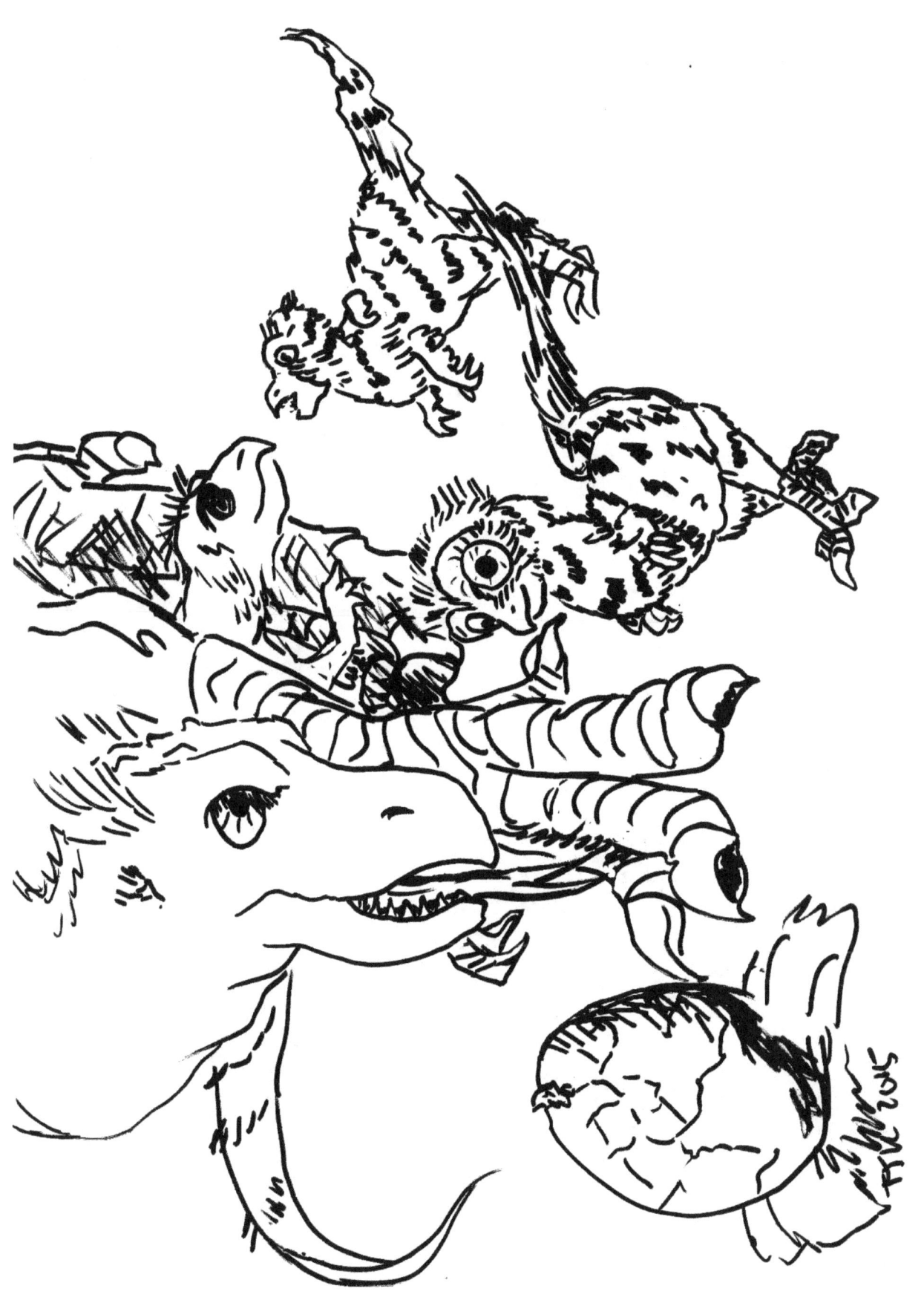

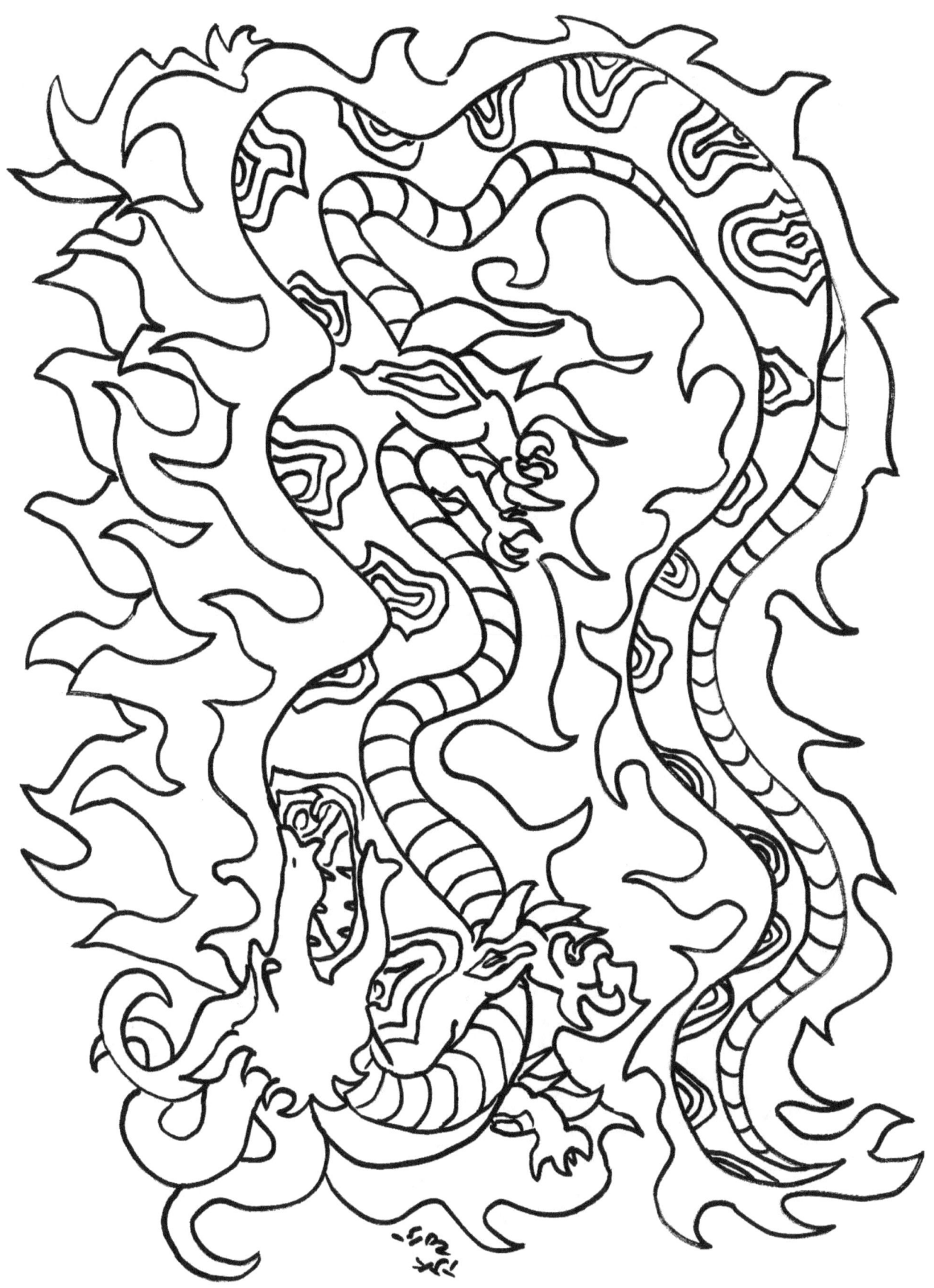

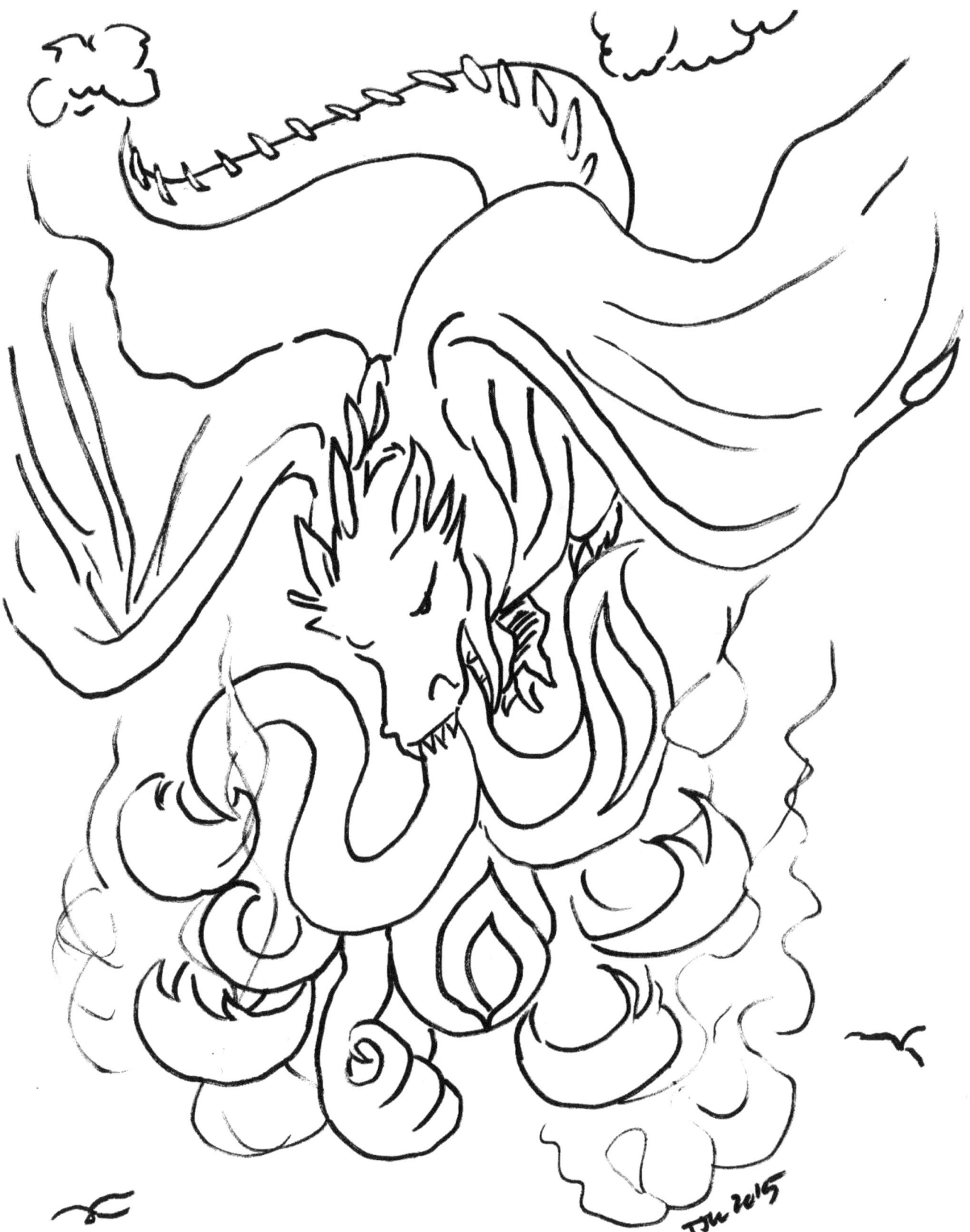

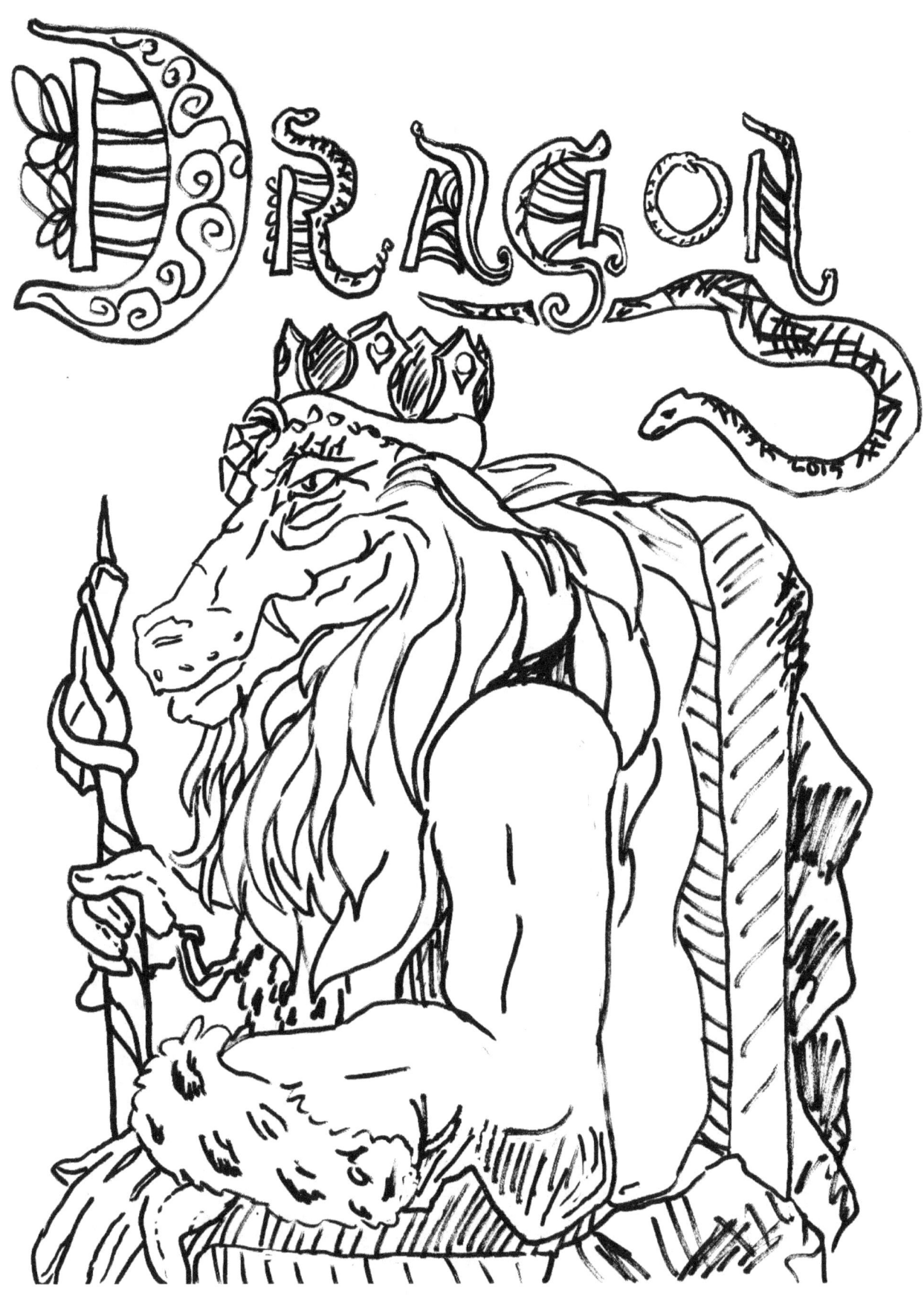

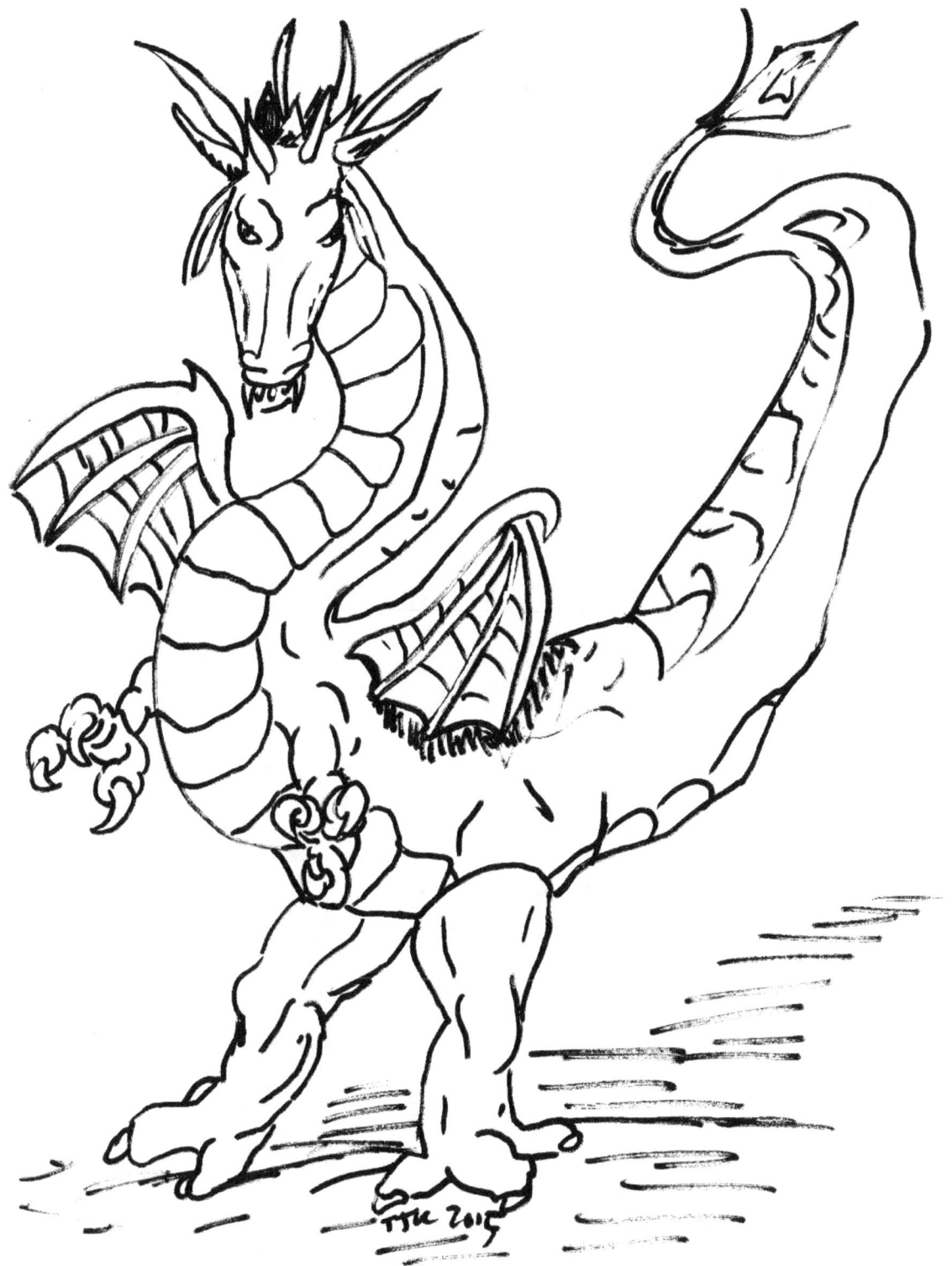

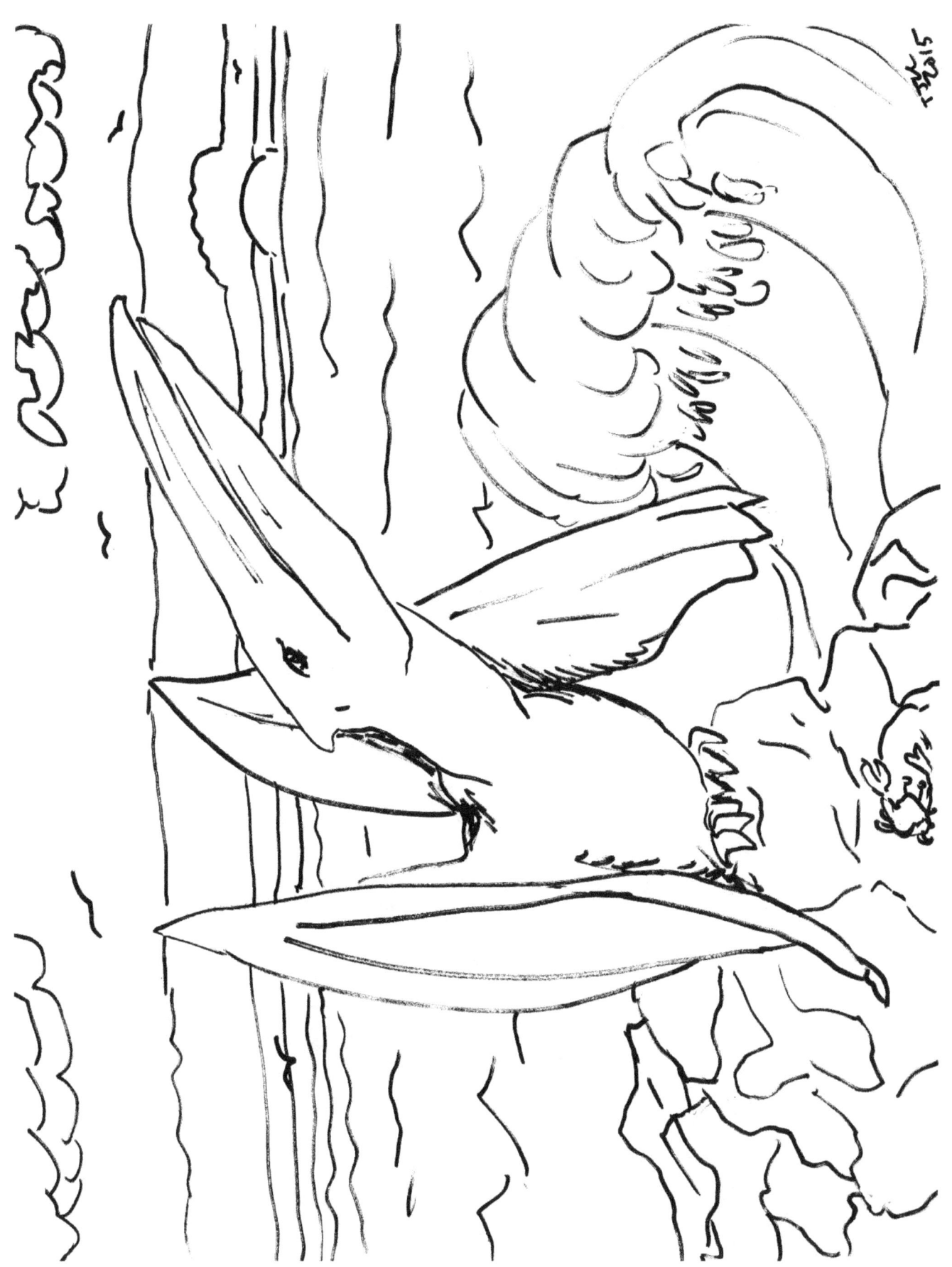

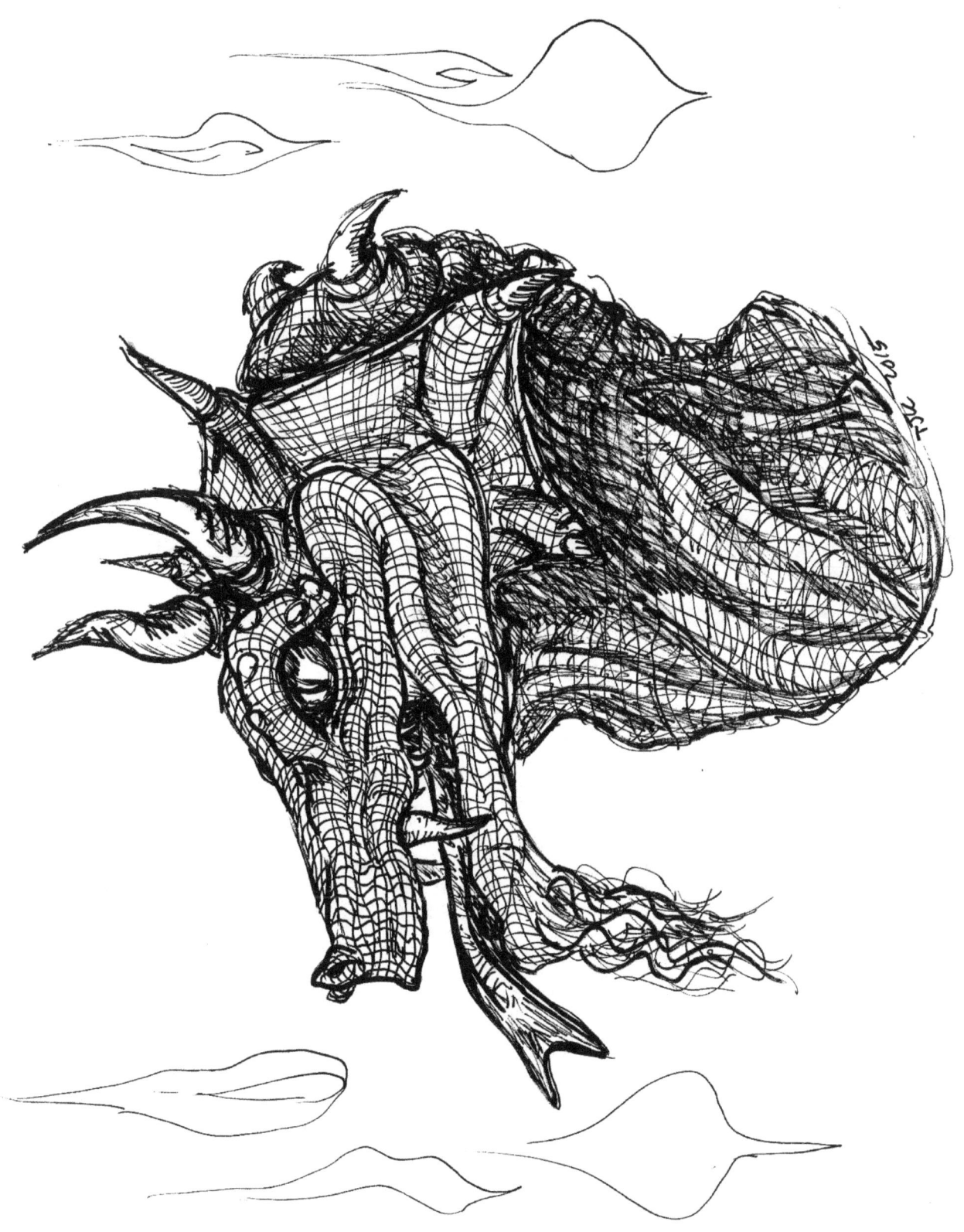

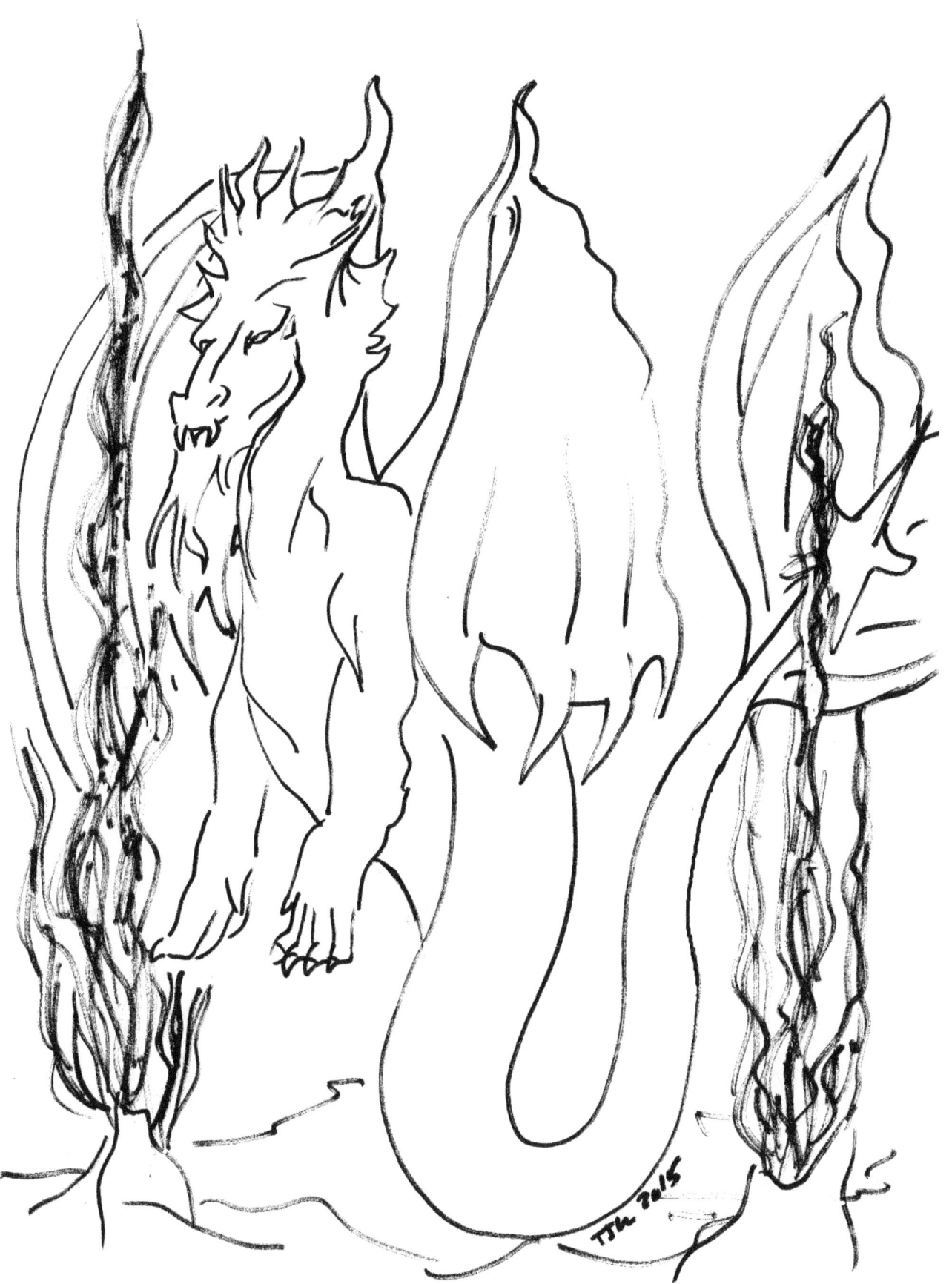

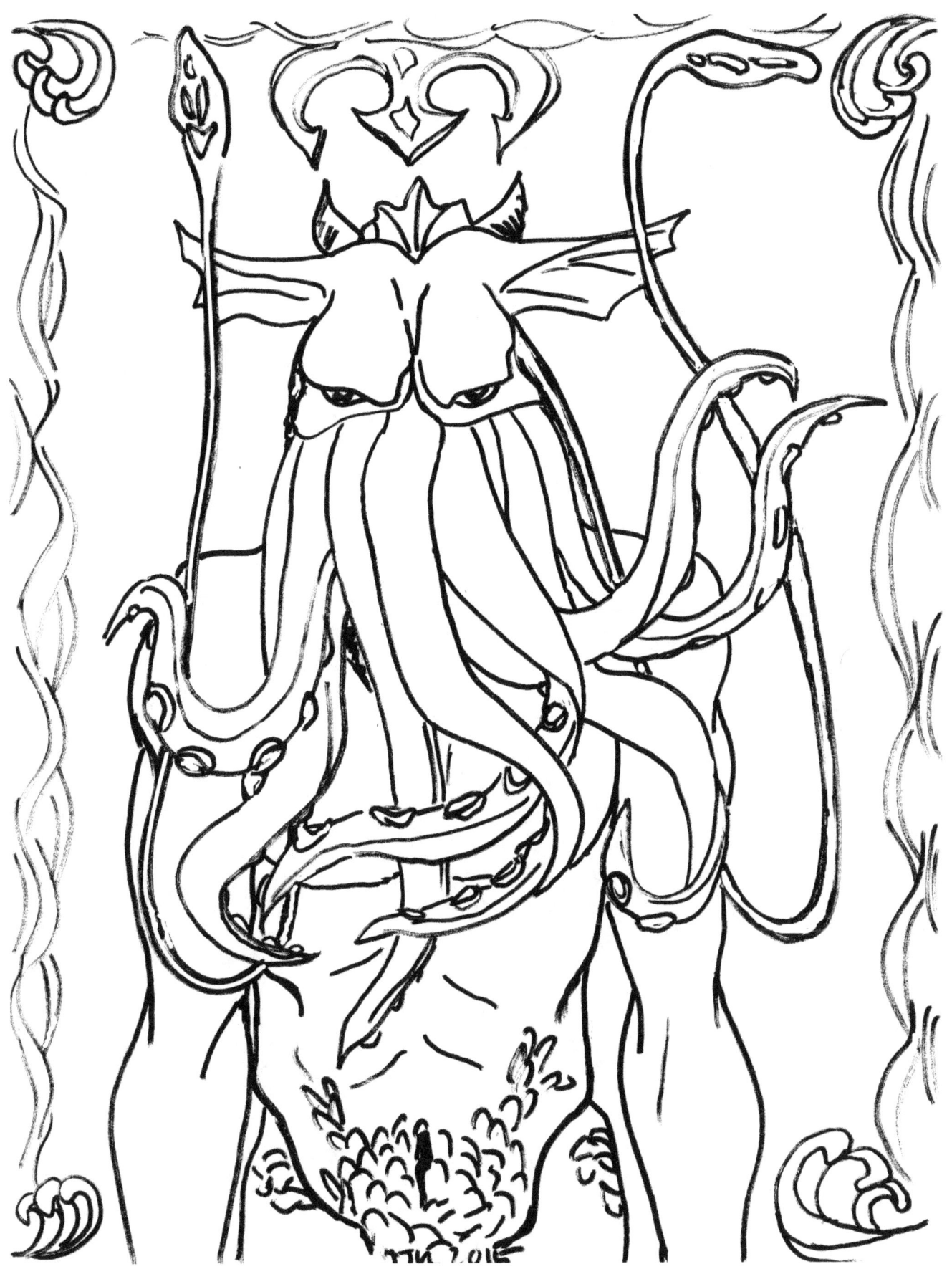

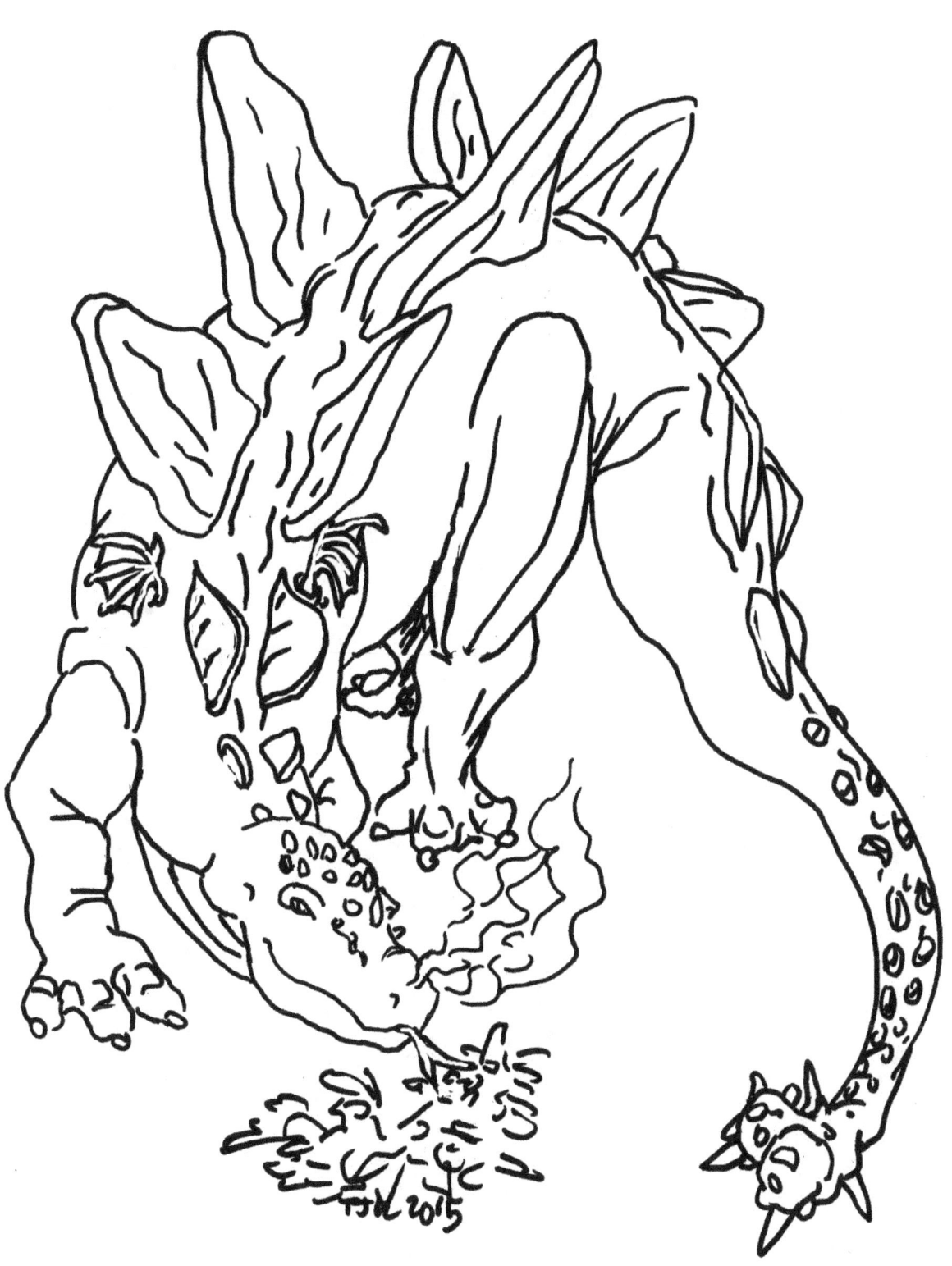

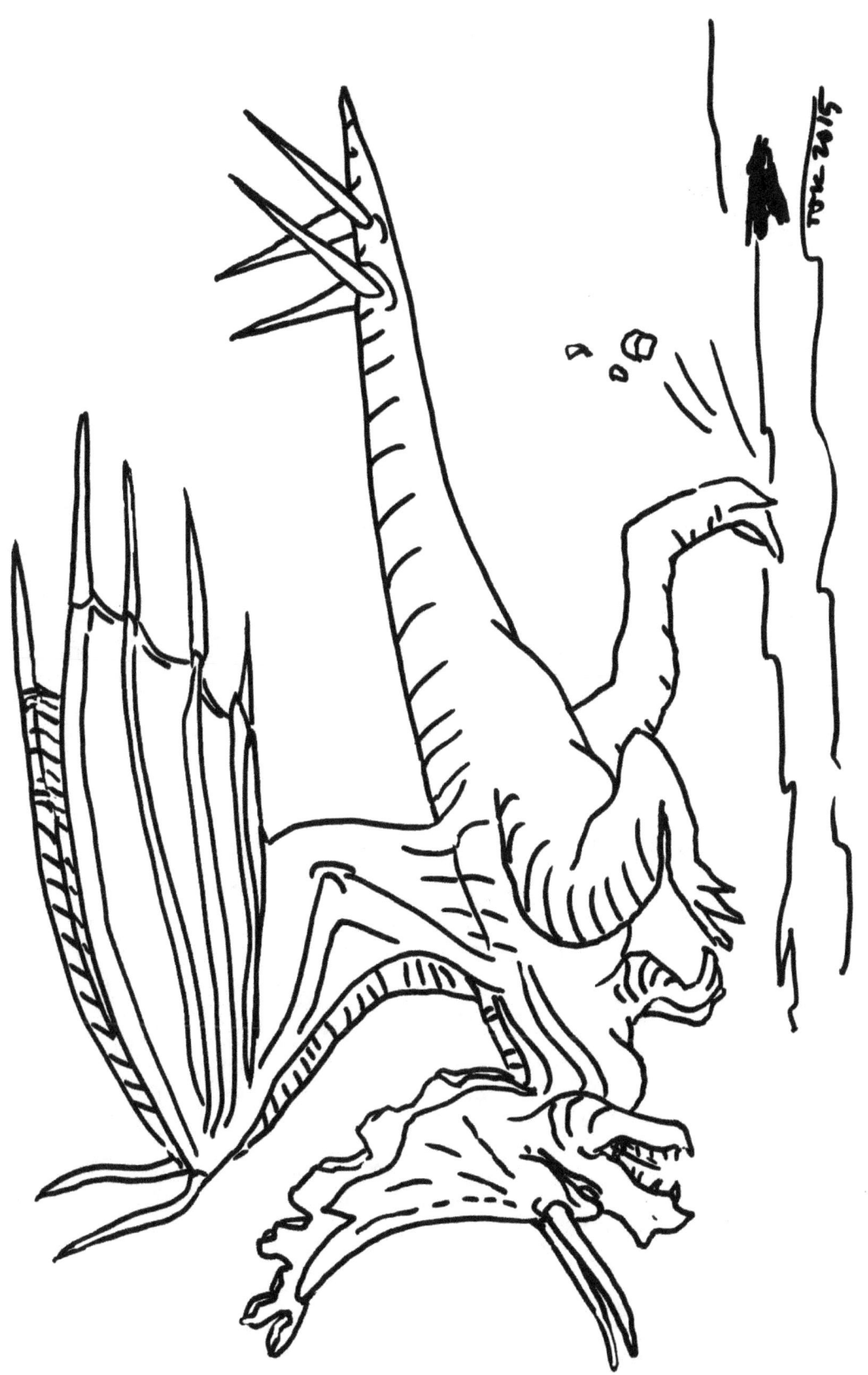

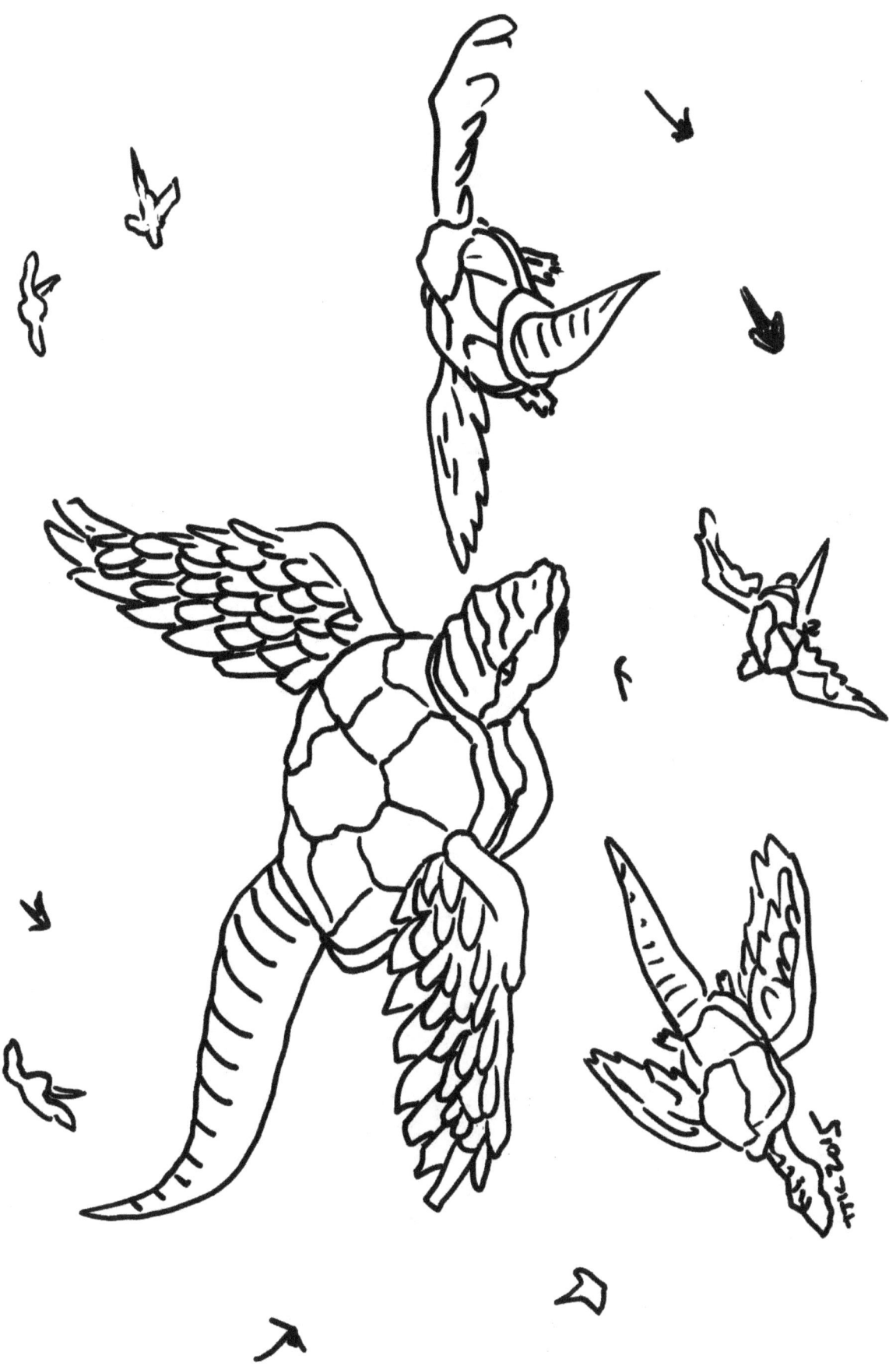

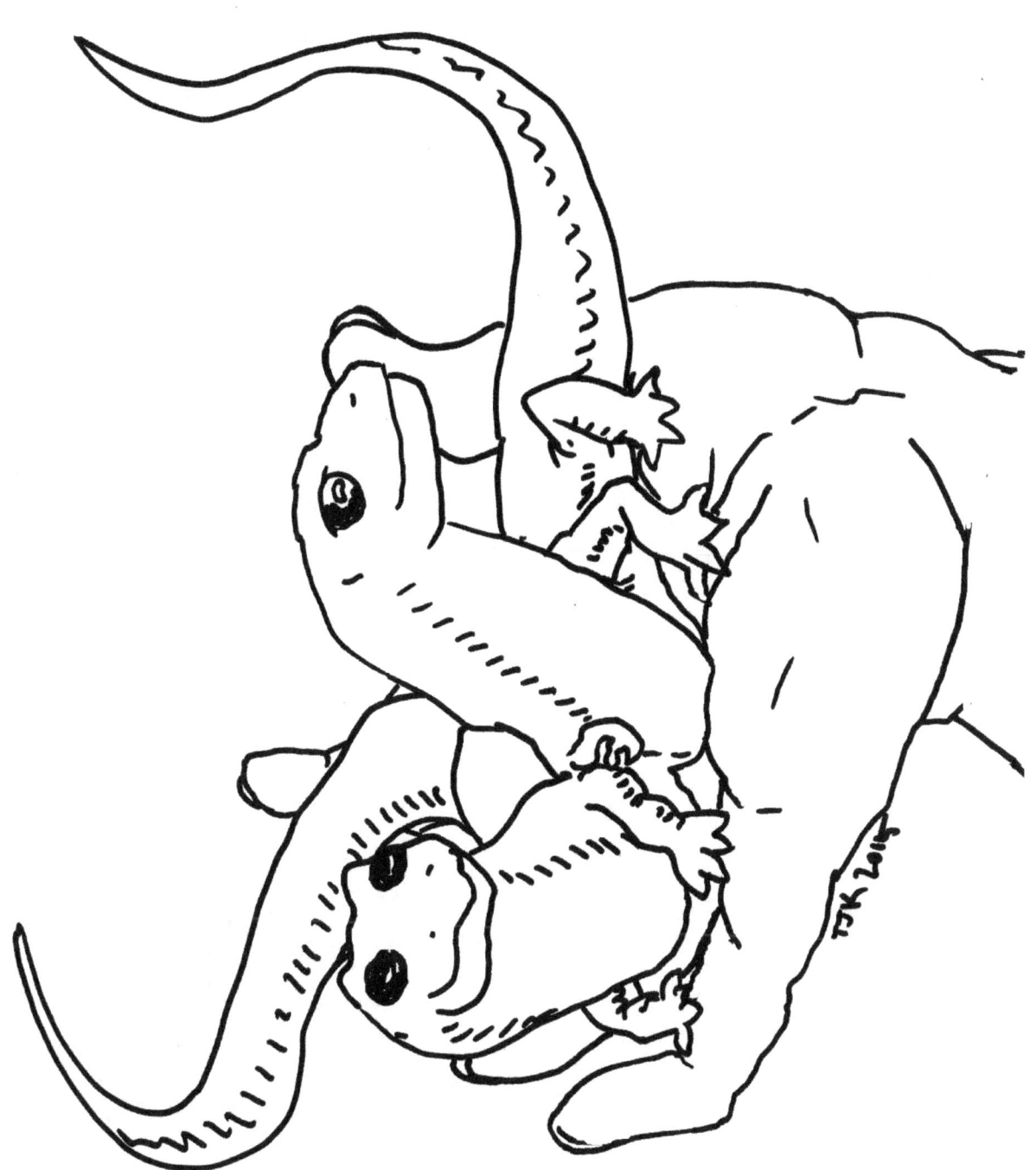

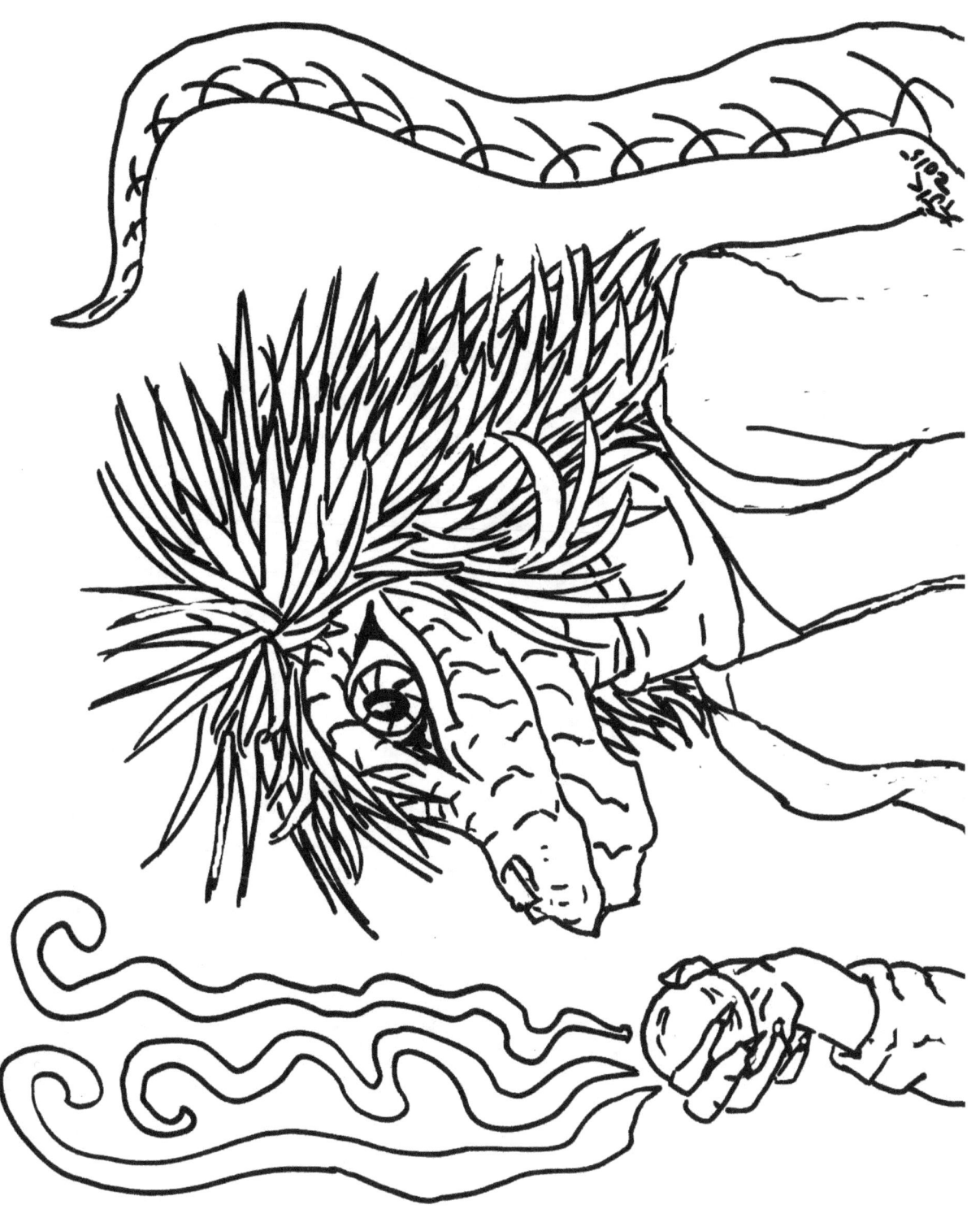

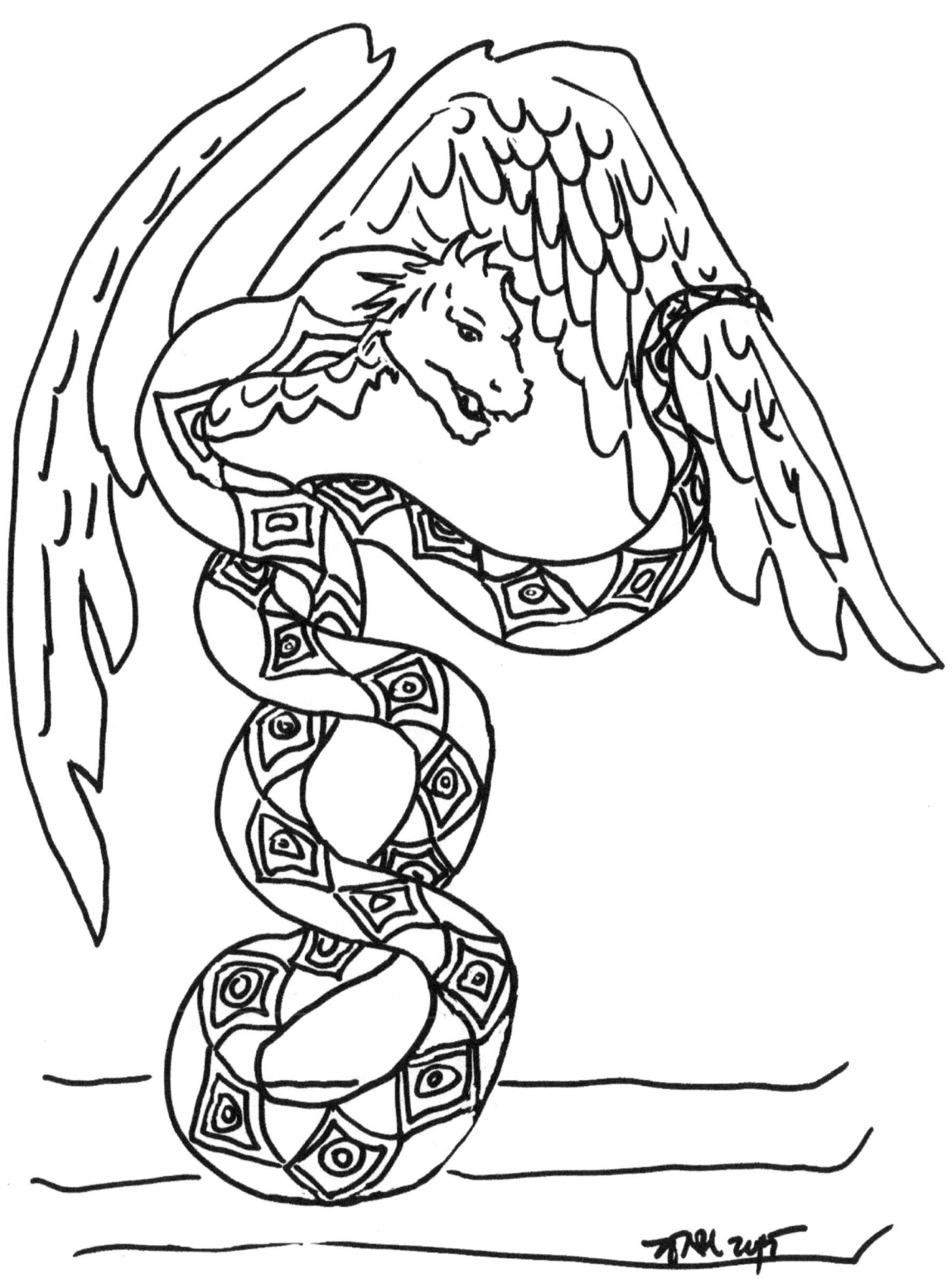

60

ABOUT THE AUTHOR

Theresa Kenyon grew up in rural New Hampshire, acquiring an interest in both art and literature at an early age. She graduated from the University of New Hampshire, Durham in 2005. For the start of 2020 Theresa will be unrolling a new healing art project. She resides in New Hampshire with various family members and a handful of cats. Active websites include youtube.com/cattheminion, cafepress.com/cattheminion, facebook.com/TKenyonArt, cattheminion.deviantart.com, and twitter.com/thecatcameback.

www.ingramcontent.com/pod-product-compliance
Lightning Source LLC
Chambersburg PA
CBHW081607170526
45166CB00009B/2861